5   12 —

Pockets
of Craziness

Pockets
of Craziness

Examining Suspected Incest

Kathryn Brohl

Lexington Books

D.C. Heath and Company · Lexington, Massachusetts · Toronto

Library of Congress Cataloging-in-Publication Data

Brohl, Kathryn.
Pockets of craziness : examining suspected incest
/ by Kathryn Brohl.

p.   cm.
Includes bibliographical references.
ISBN 0-669-24483-X (alk. paper)
1. Adult child sexual abuse victims—United States—Psychology.
2. Incest victims—United States—Psychology. I. Title.
HQ72.U53B76 1991   362.7'6—dc20   90-21847

Published simultaneously in Canada
Printed in the United States of America
International Standard Book Number: 0-669-24483-X
Library of Congress Catalog Card Number: 90-21847

The paper used in this publication meets
the minimum requirements of American National Standard
for Information Sciences—Permanence of Paper
for Printed Library Materials, ANSI Z39.48-1984.

Year and number of this printing:

91 92 93 94 8 7 6 5 4 3 2 1

This book is dedicated to my daughter, Susan Sharp,
who is love personified; my mother, Eleanor H. Brohl,
a role-model in courage; and my friend, Phil,
who has led me to abundance.

Contents

Acknowledgments

There are many friends and colleagues I wish to thank for their expertise and support: Mary Louise Nahan, Kathy Turner, Robert Dreyfuss, Ronald Gravis, Clifton Broumand, Sandy Brookshire, Diane Goldberg, Carolyne Moore, Jeffrey Gerson, Jan Cooper, Dennis Harrison, Jeanne Duffin, Nancy Davis, Tom Norris, Debra Munkasy, Eileen Jimanez, Caroline Yeardly, Kathleen Langford, Theresa Pooler, William Gladstone, Sal Fusaro, Kerry Altman, Laurie Forbes, Brien Weiss, Reva Wiseman, Lynn Moffett, Jean Albright, Gail Bathea-Jackson, and Edith Herman.

Introduction

This book is a guide for those of you who have begun to examine the possibility that you were molested as a child, particularly when you have little or no recollection of your experience.

Its purpose is to aid people who wish to delve more deeply into a suspected abuse. To that end, it provides information about putting together the pieces of an incest puzzle and prepares you for recovery work. Another aim of this volume is to dispel false assumptions and groundless fears about incest.

It also discusses the common defense mechanisms or "gatekeepers" that keep you feeling stuck in your fearful moments or those "pockets of craziness" that emerge with surfacing memories. It helps answer the familiar questions: "What's happening to me?" and "Is this recovery trip worth it?"

After reading this book, some readers may happily be able to conclude that they are not victims of incest. But if you think you may be treading on shaky ground, please understand that you do not have to start the recovery work immediately. Sometimes the first step is simply collecting information about incest.

The treatment of adult survivors of incest is a fairly new area of mental health. Although the symptoms of the incest trauma have been the subject of discussion for a long time, little was known about the recovery process until the mid-1970s. So it is not surprising that therapists who work in this field have had to blaze some trails.

Former treatment methods of diagnosing this problem and waiting for the client to talk long enough to arrive at acceptance of the conclusion can take years. Because people in crisis do not have that luxury, therapists have had to become active participants in their clients' recovery. At times, they may introduce survivors to the idea that they were, indeed, molested. The work is a multilayered process that is challenging, complex, and extremely rewarding.

While adult survivors of incest will for the most part be referred to in the feminine gender, the principles outlined in this book apply to both sexes. Many of the personal stories cited throughout the book are not, for reasons of confidentiality, direct quotes. They are, instead, paraphrases of survivors' statements.

It is my hope that, as you read this book, you will gain confidence in your reemerging truth, learn more about the recovery process, and choose safe sources who will support you on this important journey.

One last word: please be assured that in choosing to pursue your quest, you can attain a richer and fuller life.

1

Working the Puzzle

We are all working life's puzzles, of which there are many. Certain relationships, losses, or twists of fate are examples of situations that draw upon our coping abilities. Some of us have been blessed to learn how to deal with these challenges; others have not been so fortunate.

You may have been drawn to this book because you want to investigate the root of your present difficulties. That is a wise decision, a first step toward taking responsibility for discovering whatever may have inhibited you from learning healthy coping styles as a child.

If you suspect that your problems may have begun as the result of one or more forgotten incest experiences, you will be compelled to look within yourself for clues. Examining these clues can be compared to piecing together a jigsaw puzzle.

You may recall that some jigsaw puzzle pieces are easier to find than others, and that a clear picture cannot be formed until all the puzzle pieces are joined. The process of identifying yourself as an adult survivor of incest unfolds similarly when you have no recollection of incest.

Your first puzzle pieces were probably sudden flashbacks or images, unsettling feelings, or physical mental problems, which can be triggered in a variety of ways. Adult survivors of incest may initially try to ignore them.

If you are among those who have, in the past, experienced such unsettling feelings and resisted deeper investigation, you are normal. Resistance to looking more deeply into suspected abuse has many causes.

You may have false impressions about incest. Perhaps you think it involves only sexual intercourse between blood relatives. Or you may believe that, because traumatic childhood experiences occurred long ago, adults should not be affected by them. Most important, *you may fear that you will lose your sanity should you uncover the truth about your childhood trauma.* This will not happen. Remember that feelings are not facts. But there will be times you will need to rely on your intuition for help.

A Point of Reference

To dispel some myths and serve as a guide, it is helpful to know that what therapists believe is the meaning of the word *incest* is much different from the more narrow legal definition.

Sexual-assault professionals working with adult survivors define *incest* as sexual behavior such as fondling of sexual areas, intimate forms of kissing, premeditated exposure to pornographic literature and photographic posing, ongoing intrusive behavior like observing bathing habits or making sexually suggestive remarks, oral/genital contact, and vaginal or anal intercourse *between a child and an older relative or trusted caretaker who has assumed a family member role.*

Incest can occur one time only or continue over a period of years. The survivor may have had one molester or several, and the trauma suffered as the result of a childhood molestation varies from person to person.

A Form of Protection

The reason many of you do not remember your abuse is simple. One of the ways children deal with incest trauma is to repress or forget their violation. Through a natural survival process, the mind is equipped with protective coping mechanisms, which block emotions that would be overwhelming to a child at the time of her abuse. In a sense, the coping mechanisms have "freeze-dried" the experience. The trauma created by incest can be resurrected to its fullness when events in later life trigger the memory.

The following stories were imparted by adult survivors of incest before they became consciously aware of the sexual abuse to which they had been subjected. Unconscious of their primary problem, most were in therapy for other reasons. Some had been in treatment to work through alcohol or drug-related issues. Others sought help because they could not make sense of what was happening to them. For example, they wanted to know why they were startled by their sudden intuitive feelings and intense emotional pain. Wondering if they were insane, they expressed a sense of desperation. All were seeking answers. Each of them was "working the puzzle."

Beginnings

Jill

I have felt this pressure on my arm from time to time. It feels like something is bearing down on my elbow. I know it sounds strange, but I feel like my elbow is being pushed too. Recently, I could swear that someone is shoving me. I've had a doctor look at my arm, and he tells me nothing is wrong. He suggested that I might talk to someone about this sensation. I know you must think I'm weird.

Sally

Something happened to me last week that really upset me. I was visiting my brother and I was sitting in his living room watching him play with his three-year-old daughter. I suddenly got this awful feeling and found myself wanting to grab her away from her father. I felt this rage toward my brother. All he was doing was holding her on his lap, but I'd had this flash of thought that he was going to do something bad to her. Then it seems like this image popped into my mind from out of nowhere. I was about three, and I saw myself being held down by my brother and he was forcing my legs open. I feel so ashamed that I could have such feelings and thoughts about my own brother.

José

I have often felt as though I was defective. There is a small voice inside me telling me I am weak, shameful, and needy. Sometimes the voice can be really cruel. When I begin to feel good about something I've done, that voice tells me I'm pathetic and stupid. Then I do stupid things. I'm so tired of having an argument with myself. The problem is I really think I believe that voice.

Elaine

Sometimes, when I'm making love, I leave. It's hard to explain, but I just kind of float out of my body. I'm not there and my boyfriend asks me what's wrong. It's happening more often these days. It's not him. I guess I feel ashamed of myself for making love, but I also spend a lot of time fearing that I'll lose my boyfriend and will never find anyone who will love me. Why do I feel so desperate?

Sam

At about the age of five I began to masturbate obsessively. Because it embarrassed my family, they reacted to me as if I had the plague. They told me I was bad. They also talked about it among themselves, wondering aloud how I could be so strange. My dad died a few months ago and since then I'm finding that I'm not only masturbating a great deal, but that I'm also paralyzed by sudden feelings of anxiety.

Helen

When I was a little girl, I was afraid of ghosts. I realize that it's probably normal for a child to be afraid of monsters and things, but I was obsessed with these ghosts. I thought they could read my mind and would tell my parents evil things about me. I even drew them in school, and the teachers would ask me why I always drew ghosts. I couldn't answer them. Recently I've been feeling their presence again. It's so disturbing and I think that if I mention it to anyone, I'll be labeled crazy.

Beth

I've been having horrible nightmares. I don't understand why they're happening now. Everything in my life is going so well. But these dreams are awful. They're always violent and they have to do with children. I'm in the background screaming and screaming as I watch a lion attack a child and then slowly tear her apart. I am helpless. I try to run for help, but my feet are weighted down. I wake up crying and I'm covered in sweat.

Joan

I have felt compelled lately to harm my baby. I know this sounds crazy, but sometimes it feels as though she's not really my child. It seems like she's not a part of me at all. We were so excited at the idea of having her and she's very easy, but sometimes when I check on her while she's sleeping I can almost envision my hands around her neck. I can't seem to control these thoughts and I don't know what to do.

Crossroads: Listening to Your Inner Voice

Each of these people was at a crossroads. Their physical or emotional pain forced them to consider their behavior or disturbing thoughts. Their usual methods of coping were no longer working.

In the early stages of piecing together their puzzles, survivors with no clear incest recollection feel very confused. How can *anyone* make sense of nightmares, flashbacks, obsessive thoughts, unusual behavior, or anxieties when it seems as though they appear from out of nowhere? If you have felt such confusion, you are in good company.

The adult survivor's strong protective instinct, which has been keeping memories repressed (forced into the subconscious mind) for years, now finds itself involved in a contest with another inner voice, or her intuition. As one survivor put it, "I really don't want to think that I was molested, yet there is this nagging feeling that something happened." Another survivor said, "I'm sick to death of my mind. Whenever I think that I might have been molested by my brother, I get a huge migraine."

If you as a survivor choose to further question your inner voice, those survival defenses will begin to crack. You may not even have a conscious choice in the matter. Additional flashbacks or feelings may continue to surface without your permission, and you will be compelled to confront them.

A Famous Casualty

Virginia Woolf, famed author and feminist, was an incest survivor who, in despair, took her life. Some think she could no longer endure the pain that resulted from her childhood molestation by her half-brothers. In *Virginia Woolf: The Impact of Childhood Sexual Abuse on Her Life and Work*, Louise De Salvo writes that, although this renowned literary figure was aware of having been molested during puberty, it was not until she was writing her autobiography that she remembered an earlier molestation at the age of six. De Salvo believes that this recollection was devastating to her.[1]

To the unenlightened of her day, Woolf's adult coping behaviors would not have indicated that she had been traumatized. Her flippant references to friends about her sexual abuse, however, make sense to modern therapists. It is common for a survivor to maintain a stance of denial against the harsh reality of her incest.

When the core feelings of pain and shame began to crack Woolf's protective shell, humiliation and self-loathing emerged. One can only guess what triggered the acute sense of despair that caused her to place a heavy stone in her pocket and walk into the river Ouse.

The goal of this book is to lead you from despair to hope. You do not need to seek a self-destructive route in order to ease your pain.

Triggers

What are the triggers that provoke disturbing memories, feelings, and behaviors that cause people to investigate a possible incest experience?

A trigger can be anything—a happy or sad event or a loss, perhaps of a job that has been one's sole identification. It can be intuitions, flashbacks, or sensory identifications such as certain smells, touches, or sounds.

Consider the following examples of triggers that provoke severe problems or hazy images in incest survivors, which lead to their asking questions about a possible incest experience.

When the Trigger Is a Happy Event

As strange as it may seem, pleasant events can trigger recall of an incest memory or cause a person to question her past. When one feels safe and happy, memories may surface. The survivor's mind has been protecting her by waiting to bring this information to the conscious level when she is best supported by outside sources to handle the truth.

Triggers vary from survivor to survivor.

Grace

It doesn't make sense. Everything in my life is going well for a change. I am in a wonderful relationship, and my work is great. But the other day, when I was visiting my parents, an event flashed into my head. I thought at first that it had something to do with the emotional abuse I received as a child, but I don't think so. The image that came to my mind was so clear. I was in bed with my parents and my father was fondling me. I was quite young. I could see his face and his hands. They were so large. Could I be making up this whole thing?

~

Pleasant circumstances do not always evoke memories. Sometimes they emerge as overwhelming fears or "phobias."

Larry

When I moved away from home, I felt so wonderful. I got away from all the crazy family stuff. My dad and mom are alcoholics. They fought a lot. In contrast, I've tried to make my home peaceful and quiet. But in the past month I find it difficult to sleep in my bedroom. I've begun having these nightmares, and I've become obsessed about checking my closet to see if anyone is there. Every time I come home, or even go to the bathroom, I look around. I look under my bed. I worry that someone will come into the house and kill me. I've recently thought about purchasing a gun.

~

Triggers may also create "compulsive" problems like eating disorders.

Jennifer

I guess you could say I'm pretty lucky. I just had my first child last year and I adore my husband, who is a very prominent lawyer. Well, about six months ago I began taking dance lessons in order to lose some after-baby weight. But it's really turned into more than that. It's become a wonderful outlet. I've always enjoyed exercising, and it's been great to really extend myself. But there's this one problem I have. I can't stand watching my reflection in the mirror at the dance studio. I'm ashamed of the way I look. I think I'm ugly. I've cut back on my food intake, but I still feel fat.

People tell me I'm crazy for being so worried about my appearance. Actually, friends have started commenting about my weight loss. They say I'm too thin now. My sister even gave me an article to read about some sort of eating disorder—anorexia nervosa, I think she called it. She's really into therapy because she claims our parents were a bit difficult. I don't know anything about this eating thing, but I decided to humor her and talk to someone about it.

When the Trigger Is an Unhappy Event

Pleasant events provide more gentle reminders than memories triggered by unhappy times. Unhappy events, coupled with thoughts of early incest, can complicate the experience to the point of overwhelming the survivor.

Rita

My husband left me for another woman. I was so confused and I became so depressed I sought psychiatric help. The doctor kept saying that my strong reaction, which continued over months, was unusual. As my emotional state declined, I began to recall certain statements my father had made to me as a child, such as, "Now, no one will ever love you. They will know you for what you are."

Sara

It was the anniversary of my rape. I knew ahead of time it could be rough. My anxiety began to get the best of me. I was literally unable to function for hours at a time. I would crawl into bed and try to sleep. After the anniversary, my panic attacks didn't stop. During these times my mind refuses to crawl out from its black hole and while experiencing these feelings I have a very difficult time connecting with the idea that they will pass. It's been so hard that, at times, I think of ending my life. Last week something happened. I was writing in my journal and out of the blue I wrote, "Jeff was not the only one." Jeff had been my rapist, but what did it mean that Jeff was not the only one?

Helen

In one year I had major surgery, put my mom in a mental institution, and then found out that my company was transferring me across the country. I've always thought that I do very well under stress, but I don't think I'm handling things very well right now. When I was little, I took care of everything. My mom had so many husbands and boyfriends who dumped on her that I ended up being her parent. Well, it seems that lately I just can't concentrate. I am simply not able to hear what people are saying to me. I just space out. I used to do this all the time when I was a kid. Well, my supervisor told me that I had to talk to someone at the Employment Assistance Program or I would risk losing my job. So here I am, and I don't know if you can make any sense of my out-of-body mind trips either.

Taking steps to consider that there may be more to a trigger than meets the eye can be the beginning of looking at previous incest experiences.

Loss-of-Identity Triggers

Survivors of incest are often great overachievers, in part because they've learned to develop a false self as a cover for their feelings of worthlessness. There is nothing wrong with achieving unless the emphasis is on constant compensation for feelings of low self-esteem. Loss of an outside identity (i.e., job or mother role) can enhance the distortion of the survivor's perception of herself.

Many survivors are vigilant workers, volunteers, and parents, but they are frequently substance abusers as well. And although they may not remember their incest experiences, they unconsciously keep themselves distracted in order to maintain an outward appearance of well-being and an inner feeling of safety. Identification with their abilities is a protective defense against their truth.

The following individuals describe what happened when they began to grieve over their loss of identity.

Carol

I'm a recovering alcoholic. When I drank, I felt more intelligent and witty, and I could forget my problems. Until the doctor told me I could die from drinking I had no thought of stopping. After all, I'd been able to hold down a very good job. Well, I started going to AA. For the first time in my life I sat down and looked at the world without a haze around myself. It felt so odd and it was so hard, like a huge loss.

I think I knew instinctively that alcohol had also been my defense against painful childhood experiences. I've been thinking lately about what those experiences may have been. When I go back to check on my childhood, though, I come up with these large gaps in my memory. I fight like hell to remember, but every time I try to go back, I get an impulse to drink. What happened to me?

Blake

> When I was falsely accused of taking money from my firm, my whole world fell apart. I had sunk my soul into its building, its growth. After all those years, I'd lost the identity of being a director and a leader. This has all been so humiliating. I'm frightened because, lately, I've been thinking of hurting myself. I don't mean suicide, but I mean like last week I actually cut myself on my leg with a kitchen knife. Why would I do that? I just don't understand my self-punishing behavior.

Many survivors report that they have intuitive feelings about an early molestation when they feel extraordinarily distressed by a seemingly harmless act. Watching a television show or smelling a cologne worn by one's abuser can bring about such unsettling feelings.

Sensory Triggers

Triggers may be subtle. For example, people reporting remembering their abuse while they are receiving a body massage, meditating, or watching a movie on television whose theme is child sexual abuse. Frequently a smell or specific object, such as a lighted candle, will cause uneasy feelings to surface.

Pete

> I was watching this documentary on our local television station about children who were molested by their stepfathers. When they interviewed the children who had been abused, I kept thinking how familiar it all felt. I really got almost sick to my stomach. It was not a normal reaction. I just felt so awful. I don't understand.

Jane

> I began doing relaxation exercises after the doctor told me it might ease the intense pain in my back. So I had been listening to some

tapes for a few weeks. One night I decided to turn out the lights, light a candle for a change, and put on a tape. As my mind became calmer, vague and hazy pictures began to come into my head. In the pictures I was very, very small and I had this kind of weird sense that an older person, possibly my grandfather, was massaging my genital area. The gauzelike picture disappeared as I jumped up from where I was lying on the couch. Since then I have tried to put that scene out of my mind, but it was so unsettling. Do you think it means anything?

Theresa

Last week I took my six-year-old to get her hair cut. The hairdresser happened to be a man who really liked my daughter. He was wearing a familiar men's cologne and it was so strong. As he spoke softly to my little girl, I felt extremely uncomfortable. There was something funny about the way he talked to her, and that horrible smell really upset me. I couldn't get out of there fast enough.

～

Difficult times can provoke thoughts of an earlier incest experience. It is not surprising that puzzle pieces can begin to come together while a survivor is in a drug or alcohol rehabilitation center or a safe hospital setting.

First Steps

Take time now to assess your feelings about what you have just read. Can you identify any triggers that may have evoked upsetting thoughts about incest? If you feel frightened by your thoughts, *please find someone you know who seems to understand you, and share your fears with that person.* It is important to remember that you are an adult and that there are resources now available that did not exist when you were a child.

Also, triggers alone may not provide conclusive evidence that you are an adult survivor of incest. Triggers set in motion certain thoughts or feelings that push survivors to begin investigating them. Asking questions is the first step in solving the incest mystery. Still other pieces to the puzzle can bring an intuitive feeling or hazy image into clearer focus.

This is also an opportunity to seek the help of a reliable mental-health professional. Your therapist can be an indispensable source for reality checking and can provide guidance at this juncture.

The following chapters describe the behavior of child incest victims, characteristics of families in which incest has occurred, and common themes among adult survivors. Recalling your childhood, family of origin, and habitual adult behavior is a start toward solving your mystery.

2

Recalling Earlier Times:

Children of Incest

Children are traumatized by incest. This chapter tells you why this is so. As you review the information, you may remember that when you were a child you had characteristics similar to those described. If you do, it can be helpful, because you may discover more important pieces to your puzzle.

"The Burned Tree"

For children who have forgotten or are unable to discuss their incest experience, therapeutic tools are available to make remembering or sharing the secret easier. In her story "The Burned Tree," Nancy Davis, Ph.D., uses symbolism to assist young incest survivors in disclosing their abuse. Imagine, if you will, why sexually abused children find this tale appealing.

Once upon a time there was a tree in the forest that didn't look green and alive like other trees. It looked as if it had been struck by lightning and had stopped growing—like someone had come and cut its branches back to stubs. Most of the trees in that part of the forest thought that it was dead, because some trees are able to stand long after the life has gone out of them. But they were wrong, because deep down inside, this tree was alive. It just didn't know how to grow and develop into a beautiful tree with leaves as the other trees had done, because it had been hit by lightning and badly burned. Sometimes after being burned a tree goes into shock and gives up the will to grow and to live and to be like other trees.

And sometimes the shock of the lightning and the storms makes a tree believe that it can't grow and that it has to stay the same, looking charred and ugly and dead.

One day a woodchuck came along and, thinking that this tree was dead, began to gnaw on it.

"Hey! Ow!" yelled the tree.

Startled, the woodchuck looked around and exclaimed, "Who's there? Who's talking to me?"

"It's ME!" said the tree. "You're hurting me! Quit biting me!"

"I can't believe it!" said the woodchuck. "You didn't look alive. You looked deader than a doornail. You looked burned and pitiful. Why, your branches are broken and you don't even have any leaves. Now, I'm a pretty responsible woodchuck and I don't cut down live trees, because I'd feel bad about that. I just figured you were dead."

"I'm NOT dead," said the tree. "I'm not even sick."

The woodchuck gave a puzzled look. "Well, if you're not dead and you're not sick, why do you look so awful?"

Sadly the little tree said, "I don't know how to grow. I don't know how to get leaves. I don't know how to look alive again, because the lightning hit me so many times, and there have been so many storms in my life that I lost the knowledge about how to grow."[1]

Helplessness

"The Burned Tree" illustrates what happens to someone who has been sexually violated. Children relate to the story because the main character, the tree, represents the helpless feelings they are, sadly, unable to express. Like the tree, a sexually molested child shows signs of trauma and lacks the knowledge to change her situation. As a result, she can become socially, emotionally, or developmentally delayed.

The Root of the Problem

Why does childhood incest create such problems for adult survivors? Why do the dormant effects of the sexual abuse linger into adulthood? It is important to answer these questions before discussing the problems it creates for children.

Missing Pieces

The incest experience disrupts normal developmental growth in a child. From birth children must master certain physical and emotional stages of development. At each stage particular tasks are accomplished. Ideally a child proceeds through these stages without detrimental interruption.

When a child is sexually molested, primary survival instincts surface. A child is not emotionally prepared to handle an incest trauma. So when it occurs, her survival coping defenses will rally to assist her to defend herself against the painful feelings created by the abuse. During this time her ability to master a particular developmental task is severely impaired. The experience might be compared to attempting to learn a skill like driving a car while suffering, simultaneously, a migraine headache and a broken leg.

For example, one of the important developmental stages for five-year-olds is to learn that they are different from their parents. During this stage, children must discover healthy ways to separate from their parents if they are to grow normally. They must learn to express different views from those of their primary caretakers without feeling rejected or abandoned by them.

A child who is molested while attempting to master this task may become so frightened (leading to repression of the assault) or feel so vulnerable that she will not want to risk losing her parents' approval by taking steps to separate from them. Thus, her developing sense of identity is disabled.

This may be particularly true if the child has been molested by someone significantly close to her, for example, her father or mother. Consequently, she may neither practice mastering this important growth stage nor subsequently integrate it into her personality. She may grow to adulthood feeling as though she is missing a special piece within herself, but she may be unable to identify what that piece is.

Trauma Issues: Secrecy, Trust, and Betrayal

Instead of developing through healthy chains of interaction like play with peers and responsible parental supervision, sexually abused children become preoccupied with trying mentally to make sense of their unnatural situation (the incest).

Through incest they are exposed to behaviors with which they are not emotionally or physically prepared to deal. Also, they have been required to participate in these acts by someone they trust. Usually the abuser is a person on whom they depended for validation about themselves and the outside world.

Because all children are self-centered, meaning that they naturally feel that they are the center of their universe, they take responsibility for their assault. They feel that they have done something to initiate their bad feelings about being sexually molested.

To add insult to injury, many sexually abused children feel a need to keep their abuse a secret. Coupled with the betrayal of their trust by a loved one, sexual abuse creates a deep psychic wound. It is not surprising that children block the experience. In order to survive their trauma, they wish the incest away, or their survival coping mechanisms actually cause them to forget it.

To compensate for this developmental gap, children who are molested often exhibit certain survival behaviors that appear out of the ordinary. They create these behaviors to deal with the severe anxiety and depression caused by their sense of feeling incomplete. Their behaviors, which are attempts at self-nurturing, are often self-destructive, because children feel a deep sense of shame and responsibility for the abuse.

Meeting Needs

Many of the needs of sexually abused children have been met through unhealthy means or not at all. Such children may associate sexually stimulating touching with the reward that usually follows it. Consequently, they may grow up to use sex as a method for manipulating others in order to get what they want.

Additionally, children who do not receive sufficient parental nurturing may assume behaviors or careers that will bring them some type of attention. The approval they seek is created not from within but from outside themselves.

The primary caretakers of sexually abused children are often not appropriate role models for acceptable styles of meeting basic needs. These children have to learn to use their survival coping skills to get what they need; they also have difficulty trusting others to help them when they feel vulnerable. Outward appearances often belie the fact that many adult survivors feel lonely and isolated from other people.

Expressions of Hurt: Comparing Your Childhood

As you read about the telltale behaviors of sexually molested children, keep your own childhood in mind. You may have developed some of the behaviors described in the following paragraphs, but this does not necessarily mean that you were molested as a child. Children may begin to exhibit unusual behaviors for biological reasons or because of having lost a loved one through death or divorce. Child survivors of other catastrophes may display the same symptoms as sexually molested children.

Thus, it is important to think about the circumstances surrounding your childhood behavior. As you consider the following information, answer these questions as best you can.

- What survival behaviors or feelings did you have?
- When do you recall having your behaviors?
- Do you remember how they were triggered?
- Do you remember how often they occurred?
- If they stopped, can you remember why?

One survivor, who had pulled out her hair for as long as she could remember, realized that she had stopped doing it at age fifteen, shortly after her uncle died. Although she had no memories of incest, this information, in addition to a review of her adult behavior and feelings, and family background, led her to believe that she had, indeed, been molested by her uncle.

Of course, actual memories of being molested are the most apparent pieces of evidence about abuse. But, as previously noted, many adult survivors have blocked those recollections. As you review your childhood, examine any hazy images that may come into your mind. If you conjure up such impressions, try not to let them overwhelm you as you read about the characteristics of molested children.

Medical Problems

The best evidence of sexual abuse is obviously that which can be gathered scientifically; although some children may have been photographed or even videotaped by their abuser, victims seldom have access to such evidence later in life. Children who have contracted a sexually transmitted disease (STD), for instance, gonorrhea or chlamydia—a disease of the erogenital tract—are likely victims of sexual abuse. Unexplained scars in the genital and rectal areas of the body are sometimes indicators of an intrusion with an object. Unfortunately, people who do not remember their sexual abuse may have been untreated or treated for an STD as young children without their knowledge. Their doctor and parents may have attended to this medical problem, but neglected to tell the child at an appropriate later date. Not uncommonly, many survivors relate stories about family members withholding such information.

Other indicators of sexual abuse are not as clear. Many therapists have been told by adult survivors of incest that they had breathing or skin disorders. One woman in therapy related that she had had asthma as a child and nearly died several times when she was between the ages of four and six. Later the woman pieced together her sexual abuse at age three by her father. Under hypnosis, she remembered her father putting his penis into her tiny, gagging mouth.

The skin disorder eczema has been reported as a childhood medical problem by incest survivors. Eczema is an inflammatory disease of the skin that sometimes appears when the body or mind experiences stress. When there appears to be no other medical cause and other life stressors have been ruled out, doctors do a service to the child with eczema by probing more deeply into any possibility of physical or emotional trauma.

Sexually molested children frequently develop other unexplained physical illnesses. They may experience recurring stomach problems, migraine headaches, and gynecological infections.

Sexualized Behavior

Children who have been molested may engage in sexualized play with other people, animals, or objects. They may draw sexual parts of the body or create sexual themes when they tell or write stories. They may touch themselves or masturbate obsessively in socially inappropriate settings.

Some of the examples of sexualized play by a molested child include fondling another person, asking someone to touch her genital area, kissing someone in a provocative manner, or molesting a younger child. A sexually abused child may indulge in sexual play with an animal.

Children frequently indicate that they've been abused by creating sophisticated dialogue or placing their dolls in erotic positions. Other examples of sexualized play include inserting objects into the rectum or vagina. Preadolescent or adolescent children may become sexually promiscuous.

A child who is unable to verbalize her abuse may leave clues through her drawings. It is not uncommon for a child to draw round shapes representative of a penis or breasts. Others draw extremely graphic pictures with violent overtones. Their drawings may resemble one another with little variation on their themes. For example, some children repeatedly draw ghosts or monsters.

Children may leave clues about their abuse when they write a letter, story, or poem. The language in their written material has sexual overtones or morbid themes.

Masturbation is one way in which children express anxiety. It is a normal sexual practice unless it becomes obsessive (repeated several times daily), or cannot be controlled in public places. Sexually abused children sometimes masturbate in the presence of others.

As you read some of the examples of sexualized behavior, do you recall exhibiting some of them when you were a child? Remember, there is nothing wrong with you if you did. You are piecing together a puzzle and pulling together as many clues as possible. If you feel embarrassed or ashamed about anything you have read so far, although these feelings are valid to you, remember that you are not shameful and you have no reason to be embarrassed; when you are ready to have different feelings, you will.

Hallucinations

Many sexually abused children report seeing or hearing people talk to them. Other children disclose that they talk to an animal or ghost. One child reported seeing and speaking with some friendly monsters during the middle of the night. Another child repeatedly told her mother to be quiet while her "friends" were talking. It is not unusual for a child to relate very descriptively a horrible-looking ghoul or vampire around her. It is important to recognize, however, that sometimes hallucinations may be a result of chemical imbalance in the brain. A thorough examination by a qualified psychiatrist is a routine form of screening for children who relate seeing or hearing unusual things.

Escape or Fantasy Themes

Many adult survivors of incest tell you that, as children, they lived in a fantasy world. They read books, wrote soulful stories, and imagined a life that helped them escape from the harshness of their abuse. Imaginary worlds serve sexually abused children by downplaying their incest.

Preadolescents or adolescents fantasize themselves in situations or roles that are beyond their capabilities. Common fantasy themes include becoming a movie star, space traveler, spy for the CIA, or wife of a rebel rock-group member. It is normal for children to fantasize, but molested children may become preoccupied with their themes or daydreams to the exclusion of school work, other forms of appropriate play, and topics of conversation. This is one way children dissociate or deny their experience, paradoxically, as a measure of self-preservation.

Compulsive Behavior

Molested children may develop a compulsion to overeat, lose an excessive amount of weight, wash their hands repeatedly, pick at their skin, or pull out their hair or eyelashes. These are just a few of the compulsive behaviors that such children repeat over and over again.

Compulsive disorders are survival coping habits a child acquires to relieve her anxiety. One seven-year-old repeatedly pulled out her hair, ate it, and vomited. After considerable time and inquiry, her therapist learned that she had been molested by her mother. Her compulsive behavior expressed her anxiety about the abuse.

Elimination Problems

Sexually abused children often wet the bed after they are developmentally capable (usually at age five) of awakening and going to the bathroom by themselves. Though there can be medical reasons for bed-wetting, a molested child rarely exhibits them.

Some children pass their feces in inappropriate places such as behind furniture. Sexual abuse may be the cause of elimination disorders when a behavior occurs at least once a month for more than six months.

Sleep Disturbances

Many molested children have nightmares with one recurring theme. A ten-year-old incest survivor reported that she'd had persistent nightmares about snakes for as long as she could remember. These dreams are quite frightening and usually awaken children.

Insomnia or sleeplessness is common in molested children, particularly when their abuse has occurred at night.

Phobias

A molested child may express excessive fear. Many young survivors are extremely apprehensive of school because they worry that they may appear abnormal or different from their peers. They may fear physical education classes because they are reluctant to undress in front of other people. Although they may not relate their fears to their earlier abuse, their anxiety at the prospect of exposing themselves in a vulnerable fashion can overwhelm them. They are also ashamed of or embarrassed by their physical form.

The feared situation or phobia is often a trigger for the child, creating a feeling that something terrible may happen. For example, a child who was molested in her bedroom at night may understandably be afraid of going to bed. Although she cannot recall the event, her unconscious has prepared her against any more violations by bringing a potentially dangerous situation to her attention through this particular fear.

One sixteen-year-old was seen in therapy because she was afraid of taking baths. After a considerable amount of time in treatment, she began to remember that her older brother had raped her in the bathtub when she was five.

Other phobias may surface when a child is witness to a ritualistic act like kneeling or lighting a candle. Some molesters have been known to prepare their victims for sex by performing such acts before violating them. Children who were molested by believers in occult practices also become frightened by hearing specific words or music relating back to a sexual abuse.

There is a strong indication that a child who is phobic about visiting a relative or close family friend received some questionable caretaking. In recent years lawyers have sought to minimize such behavior by a child when there have been allegations of sexual abuse in custody battles. But it is always a very important consideration for the investigator.

Separation Anxiety

Linked to phobias, separation anxiety occurs when a child fears being away from someone who is seen as a protector or the only one responsible for the child's survival. It is normal for a baby to experience separation anxiety. It becomes abnormal for a child of seven or eight to cling to or shadow a parent in the course of a routine day. Children who were molested often worry that the nonoffending parent will experience harm. In such instances the molester may have threatened to hurt the parent or child if the child disclosed the abuse.

Regressive Behavior

When children are abused, they may fall back into old behaviors from an earlier time in their lives. The acts are expressions of self-nurturing. Children may speak baby talk, begin to suck their thumbs, seek out a favorite stuffed animal, or wet the bed.

Self-destructive Behavior

Of late, therapists have learned more about self-mutilation exhibited by children who have been sexually abused. Some examples include cutting herself on the legs, arms, or face. Other forms include sticking pins or needles under the skin. Such behavior calls attention to the child's low self-esteem and poor body image. Self-mutilation may also take place when a person has dissociated to a point where they feel extremely detached and cannot resume feeling. The self-injury may then serve as a "jolt" to reinitiate sensory experiences.

Suicide is the most tragic and appalling act triggered by incest. Many children have taken or attempted to take their lives because they saw no other way to relieve their psychological pain. Having neither sufficient communication skills nor support systems that could guide them in a positive direction, they choose a direct route to self-destruction.

Compliant Behavior

Molested children are vulnerable children. Because they have had their boundaries violated, they may have little sense of personal boundaries. They often form relationships quickly in order to feel loved. They cuddle with a strange adult, give away their school supplies if they see someone in need, and allow others to belittle them. These children become targets for further victimization. They may have few social skills, dress inappropriately in clothes too old for their years, or neglect their personal hygiene. Their poor socialization is also a reflection on the dynamics of the incestuous family, which is discussed in chapter 4.

Conduct Problems

Many adult survivors of incest report having had conduct problems while they were growing up, frequently through using drugs or alcohol at an early age or participating in antisocial activities.

Children attempt to escape an unhealthy environment as soon as they are able. They try to leave a bad situation when they are old enough to establish support systems outside the family or are physically big enough to walk away from home.

Molested children express their anger outwardly by destructive acts. They steal, set fires, throw tantrums, vandalize property, or fight. Many of them have run away from home only to find themselves with no means of support beyond selling drugs or their bodies.

A nine-year-old was setting fires in his home much to the horror of his mother. All efforts to curb his behavior did not succeed, but the fires mysteriously stopped when the mother's boyfriend left the family. A few years later, the youth told his mother that the boyfriend had attempted to sodomize him on several occasions.

Sexually abused children may hurt pets, indulge in violent play, or use abusive language to excess. An adult survivor tearfully related that when she was seven years old she drowned her cat.

Learning Disabilities

Molested children can express their previous trauma as a learning disability. They have a short attention span, appear distracted, and are unable to complete academic tasks. These children may have difficulty with classmates or teachers because of their problems.

A Time for Reflection

If you feel that the information in this chapter elicits echoes of your childhood, keep in mind that your puzzle may be incomplete. Although you may have had some of the child of incest characteristics, it is still important for you to look at other clues.

Keep in mind that it can be difficult to realize to what extent children are impacted by incest. That children have these experiences and continue to go about living speaks for their inner strength. You, too, have strengths, developed from childhood, which continue to help you as an adult.

Take time now to appreciate the child you used to be, the child who is still present within you. This may be a difficult concept to grasp, but everyone carries an inner child within, an inner child who was shaped by the events she experienced.

To familiarize yourself with her, consider reviewing some old photos of yourself at various ages of your childhood. Take time to appreciate how you as that child fought battles and survived to adulthood, doing the very best that you could.

Allow yourself to acknowledge any emerging emotions as you think about how unique and resilient you were. Give yourself a gift of appreciation by writing your inner child a letter conveying your desire to become reacquainted.

Other chapters provide information about families of incest, adult survivors, and posttraumatic stress disorder. They provide you with other puzzle pieces and enable you to complete your puzzle picture.

3

Families of Incest

Incestuous families do not function in healthy ways. This chapter offers you an opportunity to review their unique characteristics and compare them to your own family of origin.

When treating adults who have no recollection of an early molestation, therapists look closely at the survivor's childhood family, including roles members assumed, family boundaries, communication styles, family rituals, drug or alcohol abuse, and the survivor's extended family history.

As you read about the identifying characteristics of incestuous families, you may recall the role you played in your family while you think about the behavior of molested children described in chapter 2.

One Family's Story

Sue and Jack Moore met on New Year's Eve in 1948 and married the following summer. Sue, nineteen years old and a recent graduate of a girls' finishing school, was attracted to Jack's dark good looks and worldly manner. As an older man of twenty-seven, Jack found Sue to be sweet, gentle, and easygoing. A socially ambitious person, Jack believed that having a wife with the right family credentials would prove to be a safe investment. Jack, who had grown up poor, wanted nothing to do with his past.

What Sue and Jack did not know at the time they married was that their families had much in common. Although Sue's family was financially secure, it was not emotionally healthy. Sue's father, an alcoholic, was verbally abusive toward her mother, and Sue, at the age of five, was sent to live with her aunt when her mother became severely depressed. Upon returning home, Sue, an only child, became her mother's caretaker. Although there was little, if any, communication with her father, Sue spoke reverently of him in later years.

Jack's father abandoned his family during the Depression and never made contact with them again. When Jack was ten years old, he took jobs in order to help support the family. Jack's mother, who worked sporadically, was involved in abusive relationships. Jack lost respect for his mother over the years as he observed her slowly dying from alcoholism. His disappointment in his mother spilled over into his romantic relationships with women, toward whom he developed vengeful feelings. Before he married Sue, Jack had had a number of relationships, unceremoniously ending each one. As he grew older he gravitated toward younger women whose youthful appearances, in addition to their compliant behavior, were to his liking.

When they married, Jack and Sue were not wholly functioning adults, so that having a child within the first year of their marriage complicated their relationship. They named their daughter Mary Elizabeth. Their second daughter, Allison, was born three years later.

The children, both bright, attractive, and lively, were caught between their parents' unresolved childhood problems. Like many couples, Sue and Jack had expected far too much from one another, each secretly harboring the hope that the other would satisfy what their respective parents had not.

Within five years Sue became depressed. Jack's unpredictable, controlling, and often volatile behavior frightened her. Her attempts to communicate with him seemed to her exercises in futility. Jack found Sue's depression to be oppressive. He had difficulty expressing himself and felt that Sue should show more independent behavior. Lacking communication skills, they withdrew from each other. Sue assumed a kind of martyr stance and began focusing her attention on her children, especially Allison. Meanwhile, Jack became a successful businessman, a friendly church elder, and a city councilman. He also became a heavy drinker.

In later years Mary Elizabeth remarked that her parents displayed two separate sets of behavior: one for the community and another at home. She also remembered that she and Allison were often put in the position of taking care of their parents. They listened to their parents' complaints, encouraged them to be strong, and soothed one parent when the other became difficult.

As the elder child, Mary Elizabeth grew to be very responsible, while Allison became more playful and seemingly carefree. Mary Elizabeth speculated that Allison's playfulness appealed to their mother, who often said that her life had been sapped away by the births of the children. Sue lived vicariously through Allison. While Mary Elizabeth strived to gain the approval of her parents, Allison appeared to be unaffected by their opinions.

As his marriage declined, Jack began taking a special interest in his older daughter. He invited Mary Elizabeth to sporting events and club gatherings. He saw in her his wife's former eagerness to please. Mary Elizabeth thrived on his attention; by the time she was eleven years old, her early attachment to her mother had shifted to her father.

Jack's alcohol abuse increased through the years. He fell into the habit of taking a few drinks before dinner and usually rounded out the evening with several brandies.

One night, before her thirteenth birthday, Mary Elizabeth went into her father's den to say good night. When she walked into the dimly lit room, she detected the familiar smell of alcohol. As she bent to kiss his forehead, she was shocked to notice that her father was staring intently at her breasts and watched in horror as he lifted his hand to touch them. He whispered, "You're so beautiful." Mary Elizabeth stood still. Her mind was twisted in confusion and finally, when she was able to move, she fled the den as quickly as possible. Later, in her room, she convinced herself that her father had made a grave error: she decided that, in his drunken state, he had mistaken her for her mother.

Jack never spoke about the incident, but within a month he attempted to touch her again. As time passed, Mary Elizabeth grew wary of her father's looks and sexual advances. He seemed to approach her once a month. She stopped saying good night to him and never mentioned his actions to anyone. Mary Elizabeth wanted to believe that her father's gestures were caused by his alcoholism.

In the following months her behavior grew rebellious, and Mary Elizabeth subsequently encountered serious school problems owing to her resistance to authority figures. She found herself daydreaming more often, and her grades declined. She began to drink with older students and had temper outbursts at home. By the time she left for college, she was barely speaking to her parents.

Years later, Mary Elizabeth sought counseling for recurring bouts of depression. Over a considerable period of time, she came to the conclusion that her incest experience had been a major cause of her previously unexplained feelings of guilt, anger, and shame. Her depression ceased.

An Incest Myth

Unfortunately, the players in Mary Elizabeth's family are not unusual. Until recently the conventional wisdom regarding families of incest has been that only people in lower socioeconomic groups molested their children. The truth is that incest is a statement about how people relate within their family unit as opposed to where they live and how much money they have.

The Moore family had many of the characteristics of an incestuous family. Jack and Sue were self-centered and self-destructive. *More important, they had allowed the parent-child roles and boundaries to become confused.*

Family Roles

The best chances of creating healthy families occur when parents themselves set healthy examples in regard to physical, emotional, and social well-being. These essential building blocks toward adult maturity take place during various stages of childhood development. A person who enters into a relationship with another as a whole adult has most likely mastered early childhood developmental stages. Parents in families of incest deviate from healthy role models. They exhibit self-destructive behaviors that have been created by their own unresolved childhood traumatic experiences and lack of parental nurturing.

Sue and Jack Moore entered their marriage with such liabilities. When they became parents, they re-created dynamics similar to those they had known as youngsters. For example, their daughters learned to look after them, and Mary Elizabeth had replaced her mother as her father's primary companion.

Role Reversal

One of the factors in revealing families of incest is the situation of children becoming guardians of their parents and assuming responsibilities that far outweigh their psychological ability to handle them. Roles are reversed as parents become dependent on their children for emotional and, at times, physical support. Children in these families often end up parenting their parents.

Role Modeling

Children are most strongly influenced by the actions displayed by their parents. Sons may follow their father's example in families of incest by similarly molesting their own children. Mothers in families of incest often assume maternal roles with their husbands because this is what they knew as children. Family roles are confused.

The Emotionally Unavailable Parent

In families of incest one parent often remains emotionally unavailable to a child and hence the child lacks a potentially supportive role model. In the case of Mary Elizabeth, the absent parent was her mother. As a very small child, Mary Elizabeth learned that Sue was not able to teach or guide her in an emotionally healthy way. Feeling responsible for protecting her mother's feelings, she subsequently feared to reveal the incest.

Sue, consumed with her personal problems, developed a detached attitude toward her older daughter. And as with many other mothers whose children have been molested by their fathers, Sue felt some resentment toward Mary Elizabeth because Jack had, in fact, chosen her daughter's company over her own. After experiencing rejection from her mother, Mary Elizabeth looked to her father for acceptance and safety. Later she would say that she felt betrayed by both parents.

The Inaccessible Parent

Parents may become inaccessible to their children through illness or death, divorce or desertion, long work hours, or abuse of drugs or alcohol. Without an available appropriate role model who also provides nurturance and protection, a child can become vulnerable to victimization.

The Power Imbalance

Some societies continue to ignore the inherent rights of females, which leads to an imbalance of power within families. Such cultures devalue women in the workplace and in the home. Women are forced to become dependent upon males within the family because of their inferior financial and social status. In these families of incest, nonoffending mothers who attempt to separate from a child's molester are frequently ostracized.

Loose Family Boundaries

In all nonworking or dysfunctional families there is a power imbalance, and the person who has assumed the power position or role is often the one who first stepped across the invisible boundary lines of acceptable behavior. In pulling together the common incest threads, you have to consider these family boundaries or rules.

All families must draw lines or boundaries in connection with touching one another, living space, private possessions, and communication. In order for family members to feel emotionally safe and secure, it is important that these boundaries be consistent and that the individuality of each person in the family is respected. In healthy families these boundaries are discussed and handled respectfully and openly.

Families of incest change their boundaries when it suits them to and express little regard for family members' needs or wishes. Boundary rules are discussed in angry and blaming tones or may not be discussed at all.

Members may violate one another physically, by slapping, shouting, or playing aggressively. In the Moore family, the subtle crossing of boundaries occurred when Mary Elizabeth was required to assume the role of her father's primary companion. The blatant boundary crossing was Jack Moore's sexual abuse of his daughter.

Privacy

Bathrooms and bedrooms are the living spaces that seem to create the greatest boundary problems. Within incestuous families they represent clear physical lines that are crossed by molesters.

Many children report that they were molested in the bathroom or bedroom. One seventeen-year-old repeatedly asked her stepfather not to walk into the bathroom while she was taking her shower. Although he never touched her physically, he had clearly violated her privacy and committed an incestuous act.

Midnight visits to a child's room or peeking in on a child while she is dressing are ways in which a molester transgresses boundaries. Another survivor stated that she was always anxious when awakened by her father, who would come into her room for his "good-morning kiss."

Even living in close quarters, healthy families continue to honor one another. They knock before entering rooms, ask permission to borrow clothes, turn down their music on request, and respect personal papers.

Families of incest intrude on one another's physical space. Members may sleep in different places each night, friends may live in the home for periods of time, and parents may use little discretion when undressing or making love.

Enmeshment or Overinvolvement

Individuals in incest families are overly involved with one another. Parents do not appreciate their children for their unique abilities and frequently discourage them from becoming involved in outside activities. They tend to be extremely critical and highly emotional with their children. Sometimes incestuous families isolate themselves by living in rural areas or refusing to participate in social activities outside their homes.

Communication

Communication among members in families of incest is unclear, nonexistent, or false. Members often must guess what others want or need. Only fragments of information may be expressed; sometimes discussions are conducted in anger.

Inappropriate remarks may be made to children by adults. For example, a ten-year-old reported that his aunt told him, "You have the cutest little butt."

Communication in unhealthy families follows the paths of extremes. Sometimes communication becomes excessively rigid or overly permissive. Children may be required to answer "Yes, sir" after each remark and speak only when spoken to. Conversely, children may not be chastised for speaking disrespectfully toward others. Sometimes, given no guidance, they address their parents by their first names.

Keeping Secrets

Incestuous families often do not tell the truth. They lie to those outside their immediate circle while working at presenting a healthy picture to the community. Wives exaggerate or minimize their feelings about their husbands. Husbands fear discussing their personal disappointments.

Children are told that things will be fine even when they have just witnessed one parent abusing the other. Children are coerced into keeping their molestation a secret when the molester tells them that horrible consequences will occur if the truth about the incest becomes known to others.

Family Rituals

Incestuous families may fail to create family traditions or enjoy family get-togethers. Most healthy families develop ceremonies around daily routines or holidays. Members of families of incest may eat separately from one another, rarely play together, or fail to acknowledge certain anniversaries throughout the year. There is little celebration of life.

Holidays can trigger excessive behavior in these families. More alcohol is consumed, bills are higher, and people tend to become ill. Holidays become a time of violation rather than one of celebration.

Substance Abuse

When reviewing possible past incest experiences, therapists ask clients if any family members abused drugs or alcohol. The reason for this is twofold. First, the use of these substances over a period of time does influence a person's moods and judgment. Second, the coping styles of drug-addicted or alcoholic families lend themselves to keeping secrets and role and boundary confusion.

Keep in mind that, although many adults molested as children are children of substance abusers, not all substance abusers molest their children.

Extended Family Members

Therapists also review their clients' extended family histories, because the manner in which generations of families have lived is reflected in survivors' families of origin. They ask how grandparents related to their own children. They also listen for reports from their clients of previous emotional or physical abuse. They collect information about illnesses, separations, and other significantly traumatic events.

Charting Your Family

You may wish to examine your family by means of a family diagram similar to the one drawn below. Write your family members' names and a one-word description of each person. This can give you a feeling about the role you assumed in your family.

Additionally, you may recall messages that family members gave you about yourself when you were a child. How did you feel about them? How did you feel about yourself?

The diagram below was drawn by Jean, an incest survivor. Although it resembles a family tree, it carries a more powerful meaning.

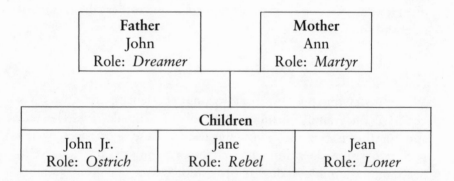

Father John Role: *Dreamer*		**Mother** Ann Role: *Martyr*
Children		
John Jr. Role: *Ostrich*	Jane Role: *Rebel*	Jean Role: *Loner*

As Jean assessed her diagram, she added other comments about her family. It proved to be enlightening for her because she was able to gain a clearer picture of why she had felt so alone as a child. She also was able to face the fact that her fantasy about having grown up in a loving and protective household was not true.

Describe your diagram to a trusted person. Discuss your family's living conditions, communication styles, and their present style of living. Do you feel you have a good relationship with them?

Moving Forward

Looking closely at your family of origin can be difficult because it may elicit unreleased painful feelings. Give yourself some time to mourn your disappointments. Remember, all this information is vital as you put together a very important puzzle. The following chapter describes common threads among adults molested as children. Their characteristics will further add to your knowledge about incest and assist you in clarifying your thoughts about the possibility that you are an adult survivor.

4

Adult Survivors of Incest

Adult survivors of incest manifest many similar characteristics. By reviewing your own adult coping behaviors and adding them to your store of childhood and family of origin information, you may be able to determine whether your present emotional unrest stems from a childhood molestation by a trusted relative or caretaker. Should you conclude that you are a victim of incest, I hope that you will begin to unburden yourself of the accompanying aftermath and set your course on the path of healing.

Carol's Story

Carol, forty-three years old, whose loss-of-identity trigger was described in chapter 1, buried memories of her early incest. A recovering alcoholic, she sought counseling because she was experiencing severe panic attacks. At various hours of the day she felt overcome with fear as her heart raced and her hands trembled.

She described her panic as "a little area in me that's separate from the rest of my life, but when I'm in it I feel like I'm crazy or gonna die."

Carol said her parents had been verbally abusive to and emotionally distant from their children. She spent summers with her grandparents. A rebellious adolescent, she began to drink when she was thirteen years old. When they reached adulthood, she and her siblings were estranged because, she thinks, they had always been critical of her.

Carol's drinking began to take its toll when she was in her early thirties. She became physically and mentally exhausted as she endeavored to maintain her heavy work schedule and her increasingly disintegrating marriage.

Carol and her husband divorced after she discovered him with another woman. Her alcoholism grew out of control and she was finally compelled to seek help after awakening one morning without the slightest memory of what had occurred the night before.

Alcoholics Anonymous proved to offer the structure and spiritual guidance she sorely needed. But as she began the twelve-step program, she was disturbed to experience periods of extreme anxiety.

Carol thought that the attacks were caused by her alcohol withdrawal. But as her sobriety continued over several months, they did not subside. She began to suspect that they reflected a childhood experience.

It was difficult for Carol to recall much of her early years, but through gentle relaxation exercises she was able to remember unsettling fragments of childhood conversations and scenes. She remembered an incident that occurred when she was three years old: her grandfather massaging her genitals. Other images surfaced during later sessions. Recalling these incest experiences seemed to compel her to want to drink. She also began to have nightmares.

Carol allowed the conflict to unfold by embarking upon the important recovery process. As she continues her recovery, clearer images of her childhood incest emerge. But her panic attacks are less severe and she does not experience them as often as she used to.

Gatekeepers or Coping Mechanisms

Carol, like all adult survivors of incest, developed coping mechanisms or gatekeepers that allowed her to maintain a sense of order in her life. Her drinking was such a defense. When she attempted to stop this self-destructive habit, a more horrendous truth was revealed to her.

Coping mechanisms, often physical or mental disorders, are attempts by the survivor to overcome the horror of her abuse.

As you review these common threads, you may begin to sense a familiar pattern in your own life. Think about when your traits appeared, their intensity, and what had occurred in your life prior to their onset. Be careful not to isolate one characteristic. Rather, focus on sets of problems. The information is especially significant if, for a time, you have had hazy visions or intuitive feelings about an abuse.

Physical Problems

Body-work professionals believe that the human body has full recall of its previous traumatic experiences. It makes sense then, that survivors of incest carry their childhood physical problems into adulthood. Physical problems include

- gynecological conditions
- breathing conditions
- serious skin rashes
- back pain
- stomach ailments
- severe headaches
- physical pressure

Clamping

One of the most common gynecological problems seen in incest survivors is vaginismus or the "clamping disease," which is a spasm of the vagina. Not actually a disease, it occurs when an object such as a penis enters the vagina.

Vaginal Infections

Frequent vaginal infections or difficult periods may also indicate sexual trauma. Survivors can experience rectal pain due to scarring from object penetration.

Asthma

Asthma has been reported as a frequent breathing disorder in adult survivors of incest. This problem may stem from a time when they were forced to participate in oral sex.

Eczema

Eczema and other skin rashes recurring over a period of time give clues about an early incest experience. One survivor related that she had severe rashes when she was a child. As memories of her incest surfaced, they reappeared.

Back Problems

Muscle spasms in the back are also reported by survivors. These problems cannot be traced to a particular accident or illness.

Stomach Ailments

Stomach ailments such as colitis and ulcers are often reported by adult survivors of incest. Stomach problems quite often relate to stress experienced in a survivor's early childhood and adult life.

Headaches and Dizziness

Many survivors complain of severe headaches for which there appears to be no physical basis. Such headaches occur at the onset of adolescence and continue through adulthood. Not surprisingly, they become most pronounced during times of stress.

Physical Pressure

Interestingly, some survivors feel physical pressure on various of their body parts. For example, one survivor said that she often feels pressure on her inner thighs. She is careful to keep her legs crossed to alleviate some of the discomfort. Others report pressure on the upper arms, forearms, and neck. Still others say they have felt a push or shove. The people reporting these symptoms were otherwise physically normal and had no medical reasons for their conditions.

Mental Problems

A myriad of mental disturbances are caused by incest. They were identified in the late 1800s by Sigmund Freud as he worked with women who reported that they had been molested by a family member. The primary mental problems from which adult survivors suffer include

- depression
- severe mood swings
- anxiety
- compulsive disorders
- phobias
- hallucinations
- sleep disturbances
- flashbacks
- dissociative problems
- addictions

Depression

Depression can be identified as homicidal feelings turned toward oneself. It can be further described as feeling powerless to change one's circumstances. The anger created by those helpless feelings is, again, directed toward oneself.

Depression is present in child incest victims because they always feel responsible for their abuse and helpless to express their anger toward their abuser, feelings they carry into adulthood. Many survivors have had suicidal thoughts or have actually attempted suicide. Still others, sadly, have completed the act.

Mood Swings

Survivors experience severe mood swings that cannot be traced to a biological cause. One person said, "I feel like I am on a roller coaster. Just when I think I've struck a balance, I hit a new high or low."

Anxiety

Anxiety is a state of extreme worry. Similar to phobias, anxiety centers on a fear about projected harm to oneself or loved ones. Physical signs of anxiety include sweaty palms, difficulty catching one's breath, and a racing heartbeat. Anxiety may be the result of having been prey to unexpected sexual violations in childhood.

Compulsive Behavior

A compulsive behavior is an action one feels forced to repeat over and over. Examples include hand washing, cleaning, cutting oneself, pulling out one's hair, using laxatives, or seeking excessive sexual gratification. Eating disorders like bulimia and anorexia are also examples. These behaviors are attempts to regain control of one's life and to purge oneself of the feeling of shame.

Phobias

Phobias are excessive fears or feelings of dread. For example, survivors may fear being alone or being physically placed in compromising places. They may react violently to being tickled or pinned down during harmless play.

Hallucinations

Survivors may experience auditory or visual hallucinations. Auditory hallucinations can include booming reverberations, someone calling, footsteps, or children crying. Visual hallucinations can include seeing shadowy figures, usually out of the corner of the eye. Survivors most often became aware of these figures when they are resting.[1]

Sleep Disturbances

Sleep disturbances can manifest as nightmares with death or violent themes. Such dreams awaken survivors, who are shaken and perspiring. Nightmares reflect the unconscious mind's attempts at control and mastery of a survivor's early trauma. As she begins to heal, the survivor has dreams in which she becomes angry at or defeats her aggressor physically. This is healthy progress, because it indicates that she is attempting to recapture her personal power.

Flashbacks

These images appear as pictures in the mind of the survivor. They emerge suddenly, leaving survivors feeling overwhelmed and disoriented.

Dissociation

Dissociation protects the survivor by denying her painful experiences. Daydreaming, intellectualizing, splitting, viewing ideas as all good or all bad, projecting personal experiences onto other people, assuming one or more different personalities, and memory lapses are all symptomatic of dissociative behavior.

When survivors begin to acknowledge incest experiences, they sometimes fear that they may have multiple or fragmented personalities. In therapy they may, indeed, discover that personality fragments have split off from their core personality. Healing occurs when the survivor is able to identify, befriend, and manage the fragmented personalities, which, in turn, leads the survivor toward becoming less frightened of them.

Addictions

The abuse or habitual use of alcohol and other addictive substances is common among adult survivors of incest. Most people identify substance abusers as those who use drugs like cocaine, marijuana, heroin, or LSD. While these are among the substances used, survivors also abuse prescription medications such as muscle relaxants or mood elevators. Nicotine is a widely abused substance. Laxatives may also be abused.

Many adult survivors who begin using substances at a fairly early age stop when they must choose between living and their addiction. This proves to be a tall order for someone who is faced with yet another emotional struggle in the form of recovery from an incest experience.

Self-destructive Behavior

Self-destructive behavior carries three basic themes:

- low self-esteem
- struggle
- lack of trust in self and others

Low self-esteem emerges as self-punishing behavior. Struggle surfaces as poor impulse control and phobic behavior. Distrust appears as the inability to form intimate relationships.

Low Self-esteem

Poor self-worth is a deep feeling within a survivor. Adult survivors of incest believe that, if others truly knew them, they would be unmasked as the unlovable people they think they are. One therapist cites the example of a beautiful woman who sincerely felt she was unattractive.

Self-destructive behavior is typical of many adult survivors who learned from their early-life violations to feel like "damaged merchandise." As a result, shame and humiliation become dominant feelings in these survivors.

HIGH-RISK BEHAVIOR. Adult survivors may place themselves in such potentially risky situations as prostitution. Other high-risk behaviors include choosing dangerous occupations, participating in daring sports, or performing reckless acts (i.e., driving too fast).

Their compliant personalities and unconscious wish to die lead them to meet and trust strangers. Because they befriend unscrupulous people, they are apt to become rape or murder victims.

SELF-MUTILATION. Many survivors punish themselves by inflicting physical harm to their bodies. They may cut themselves or binge on food, then force themselves to throw up, or starve themselves in order to feel more attractive. Tattooing or piercing earlobes in several places may offer evidence of self-mutilation.

Struggle

Survivors tend to complicate their lives unnecessarily. They adopt impulsive rather than self-empowering coping styles, having learned these mechanisms when they were children in order to guard themselves against further victimization.

Survivors frequently place themselves in crisis situations, such as quitting a job before they have found another. They can live at a high anxiety level, which can inhibit them from setting clear goals. Completing simple tasks can feel complicated.

Survivors tend to be plagued by money problems and to overcommit themselves financially. To please others, they extend themselves beyond their capabilities as well.

Trust

Incest survivors have difficulty establishing trusting relationships. Many enter into multiple marriages and suffer abusive partners. They may become involved in unattainable relationships (e.g., married men) or, conversely, choose to isolate themselves from members of the opposite sex. They may themselves be untrustworthy because they fear closeness.

Survivors have difficulty identifying their feelings. They do not know what makes them content or what their physical or emotional needs are. They do not know how to ask for what they want, because doing so releases fears of rejection or punishment.

Survivors tend to think of relationships in terms of all or nothing. They are apt to place all their emotional "eggs in one basket," hoping their partners will erase the pain that can be eased only within themselves.

Struggle for intimacy with others emerges because survivors tend to distort their expectations in relationships. They do not accept partners realistically. They may be overly giving or withholding of affection or have difficulty expressing themselves verbally because, as children, they learned that self-expression meant rejection.

Survivors Who Abuse Others

It is important to note that those who have been sexually abused as children may in turn abuse others physically or sexually. The majority of sex offenders have themselves been violated.

While the abuse of others may be an indication that a person is an adult survivor of incest, it should be added that there are no studies which speak to the numbers of people who have been molested and have chosen *not* to be abusive.

Reviewing Your Adult Coping Defenses

The adult coping styles of incest survivors can become so severe as to evolve into life-threatening situations. For example, one survivor consistently brought men back to her apartment after meeting them for the first time at a bar. Another engaged in extramarital affairs to the extent of contracting AIDS.

Take a moment to inspect your own behavior carefully for similarities to any of those described in this chapter. If you identify with one or more of them, you may find it valuable to examine their origin and how they developed into recurring themes in your life.

It is normal to feel uneasy if this information about children, families, and adults begins to seem familiar to you. If your feelings frighten you, write down your thoughts, stop reading this book, and take some time for another activity.

Keep in mind that you may begin to experience images of an earlier time. When this happens, participate in a physical activity, perhaps jogging, cleaning, or walking, to enable you to disengage yourself from feeling as though you are reliving an experience.

To help you deal with your information, further chapters assist you in choosing a recovery support team and give you valuable advice about making a commitment to healing from your early trauma.

5

Pockets of Craziness and Gatekeepers

This chapter addresses the feelings of high anxiety or "pockets of craziness" that may have compelled you to investigate your childhood incest. Tied to your defense mechanisms, or gate-keepers, these feelings of terror have probably surfaced at other times in your life. Some survivors describe these moments as panic attacks and, in fact, they often are accompanied by a physical reaction such as rapid heart rate, dizziness, or sweating. You may have attempted to ignore them through drugs, sex, or fantasy. Unfortunately, they return to remind you that you need to look at the root of their origin.

As you begin to piece together your incest puzzle, you may be subject to one or several of these agitated states. The feeling can be compared to "choking" or other intolerable suffocating sensations associated with rage, irritability, sleep disturbances, flash-backs, or other unsettling experiences. While you are in the midst of this anxiety, you may feel as though you are going crazy or dying.

These strong fearful emotions are frightening to someone who cannot identify their roots. Considerably different from normal worry, they are perceived as a separate feeling from normal fear and are overwhelming while they are manifesting themselves.

Pockets of craziness are also linked very closely with shame and self-loathing. Shame is one of the cornerstone feelings of adult survivors of incest. A child's shame about experiencing a sexual trauma is strongly associated with the anxiety of being molested by a trusted person and the secrecy surrounding the assault.

Post-traumatic Stress Disorder and Adult Survivors

These feelings constitute what mental health experts have come to identify as posttraumatic stress disorder. They represent an acute reaction to childhood experiences.

Some scientists believe that this problem has a biological basis.[1] In other words, the terror created by an assault can trigger biological changes in the brain leading to an increase in the secretion of specific hormones that mobilize the body to meet an emergency.

When the body is in such a state, the survival instinct emerges to run/escape or fight. The brain oversecretes these brain chemicals so that the survivor remains susceptible to emotional triggers. In later life she may feel the same terror she felt as a child even when she has not experienced a physical threat.

Scientists believe that the inability to stop the initial trauma from occurring increases a person's tendency to develop this disorder. The event can be triggered by any number of stimuli later on, leading to reexperiencing the trauma. This may be why adult survivors of incest continue to feel pockets of craziness.

A Survivor's Response

The body may also protect a survivor of incest trauma to feel numb or block the earlier experience, according to those who research this disorder.[2] This may be the reason children do not remember their abuse or behave in a nonaffected way immediately after the assault.

Adult survivors of incest are not the only people who experience posttraumatic stress disorder. Anyone who has sustained a life threat that is generally beyond her control can experience the effects of the disorder. Vietnam veterans and Holocaust and natural catastrophe survivors can become troubled as well.

These episodes of great panic or anxiety, then, are the body's normal reactions to abnormal situations. It is not unusual for someone to have these reactions following an incest experience.

And again, these responses can be triggered immediately after an assault or much later in life.

For example, Carol, an incest survivor whose grandfather had molested her, was triggered into terror by being physically exposed to old men or simply by viewing them on television. To control her pockets of craziness she began to drink because alcohol offered her relief from her pain. Preoccupied and numbed by liquor she could continue to block her discomfort. Thus, her defense mechanism, or gatekeeper, was her drinking. When Carol became sober the flooding memories forced her to face her incest.

Other adult survivors of incest describe their feelings when they experience their pockets of craziness.

Shawn

"When I am in the middle of one of my "spells" I cannot believe that it will pass. Everything appears to be much more than I can handle." Shawn's trigger was a flashback of her early assault.

Pam

"Talk about panic. I can't stand to stay in one place when I'm this way. I have to run from or to something. My usual response is to make a plan to move. I have gone so far as to call movers during these times." Pam's trigger occurs when she ends a relationship.

Kris

"I go to bed and cry. I may spend the entire weekend in bed with the covers over my head. I'll watch movies on television the whole time and refuse to leave my house. I'm afraid to drive or do anything that could be dangerous." Kris's trigger is being criticized by her boss.

Kevin

"I feel as though I'm losing my mind. I cannot tolerate how I feel. That's why I began to drink. I know it's tied to something in my past, but it's like I'm never going to feel any different." Kevin's trigger occurs when he visits his parents.

Natasha

"You know, for years I thought there was something really wrong with me because every time I felt so anxious, I would begin to think about stuff that happened to me when I was a child. I just had these vague feelings about someone hurting me sexually. Then I would crawl out of my mood and forget about it." Natasha's trigger is when she is by herself for a few days.

Annabelle

"No one can describe the uncontrollable rage and humiliation I feel when I'm experiencing these moments of madness. I feel as though I could tear out my hair. It seems as though I'm terribly guilty about something and feel such horrible hatred toward my-self." Annabelle's trigger is talking to angry people.

Juan

"Basically I despise myself. I think I am shameful and bad. I get into these times where I seriously want to hurt myself. One time I almost died after I drank a fifth of liquor and proceeded to set the house on fire." Juan's trigger is making love to someone he cares for.

Mia

"How would I describe my pockets of craziness? Pure hell. It seems as though all my emotions are being hung out to dry and I can't find comfort from anyone or anywhere." Mia's trigger is cutting a man's long hair.

Ingrid

"As I was working through my incest recovery program, I experienced a number of anxiety times. It seemed as though they would never subside, but as I faced them and told myself they would eventually pass, they did. It was more difficult than anyone can imagine, though." Ingrid identified several triggers, which included reading articles about child abuse, certain sexual positions, and talking to family members.

~

More About Gatekeepers

Gatekeepers—defense mechanisms—are created as a protection against pain. *Therefore, those who suffer trauma* come by their gatekeepers honestly. Gatekeepers are triggered or emerge because of the unconscious memory of incest.

Everyone develops defense mechanisms in order to grow into adulthood and sustain a normal way of life. It is healthy to be cautious in new surroundings or fearful of driving on slippery roads. However, adult survivors of incest often develop gatekeepers that prevent them from facing their fears and overcoming their problems.

While Carol's alcoholism served to protect her until she was strong enough to face her incest, it also kept her stuck. Unless Carol had taken steps to stop drinking, she would have been unable to fully realize and deal with her anxiety and panic. At some point it is necessary to examine those gatekeepers that continue to hold you back from coming to terms with your early assault.

The cycle of these feelings repeats itself. Carol's cycle is illustrated below.

Trigger————————Pocket of Craziness————————Gatekeeper
(elderly men)   (panic attacks)   (drinking)

When Carol discarded her gatekeeper, she was forced to deal with her panic attacks. She was then able to identify the occasions when she became panicky and, later, focus on her abuse.

Sometimes survivors get rid of one gatekeeper only to substitute another one that is just as destructive. One survivor was an overeater, but later substituted starving herself for her compulsion to eat. Her new habit perpetuated her cycle of avoiding pain.

Take a moment now to identify your gatekeepers. They may include some that have been listed here by other adults who were molested as children.

- Compulsive spending, exercising, eating, working, etc.
- Anger
- Addiction to substances or relationships
- High-risk occupations or hobbies
- Depression
- Fantasizing
- Religiosity
- Reading
- Preoccupation with physical illness
- Crying
- Self-mutilation

Overcoming High Anxiety

The only prescription for coming to terms with your incest is to face it. There is no way to avoid emotional pain while healing from your childhood experience. So think about the self-destructive habits that have kept you from working through your pain.

As you review your defense mechanisms or the gatekeepers that got you to this stage in your life, remember that they served you for a reason. They kept you alive during the time you were unable to cope with your truth. It is important to view them as friends rather than enemies. But as with potentially harmful friendships, it may be best to let them go.

As you contemplate letting go of a gatekeeper that has kept you functioning, but is now keeping you down, use your recovery support team (see chapter 11). Discuss your intentions of ridding yourself of your gatekeeper with your team. Ask for help. Alcoholics Anonymous devised the sponsor system for those who wish to maintain sobriety while working through the twelve-step program. You need a sponsor or coach to help you deal with your incest and shed your self-destructive habits.

Don't Give Up

Your pockets of craziness may seem to increase as you delve more deeply into your suspected incest. Their roots are very deep, but do not give in to former methods of coping. *Instead, as you begin to sense an oncoming panic attack or other period of high anxiety, tell yourself that you will survive the experience.* Alert one of your support team members (see chapter 11) in case you need to be with your person during this time.

Remember to repeat to yourself that you will get through your intense feelings. You will. You may feel as though you will never again be calm or at peace, but you will. After your intense moments have passed, you generally feel exhausted and perhaps even peaceful. But the trick is to sustain during your panic periods the knowledge that you will live through them and that they will eventually go away.

Becoming Clean and Whole

The fact is that your panic attacks do subside. While you may feel their intensity as you begin to face your earlier assault, they gradually become less severe and occur less often. It is difficult to have faith that the struggle they cause in your life will lessen. However, once you deal with your incest, the pockets of craziness generally go away, leaving you feeling clean and whole.

Some people report that these times reoccur whenever they must deal with another hidden memory. Instead of anticipating them with dread, survivors learn to use them as thermometers to gauge when they need to attend to a concern.

Panic periods may continue for years or vanish after a few months. It depends entirely on the incest experience and the survivor's willingness to walk through her recovery process.

Remember that you can always recall your gatekeeper should you so desire. It does not disappear. You can invite it back into your life. But as a wise person once said, "When one becomes absorbed in a habit far more pleasing, the old habit falls away."

As you internalize the support from others and feel safe enough to express yourself, your gatekeeper will fall away.

At times it will be extremely difficult to let it go. You will want to feel numb again, just as Carol did when she had to fight the urge to drink. But as you know yourself more fully and appreciate your own courage to face your abuse, you will find that you no longer need your gatekeeper.

Facing Your Fears

You have been challenged to dive deep within yourself to uncover feelings and knowledge that have been buried for a very long time. This is not an easy task. But you have shown yourself to have strength when you decided to learn something about the nature of incest. It is difficult and can become frightening.

Remember that there are people who can assist you. Although your tendency may be to isolate yourself, think about how helpful others may be as you face your fears. If you have one person you can trust with your information, use her as a sounding board.

It is important to know that when people feel fearful, ideas may become distorted. Your fears may be distorted, so it is good to check out your thoughts and feelings with another reliable human being.

Once you decide to work through your recovery, have faith that you will survive and that you can become the person you most respect. The reality behind that mask of fear is manageable and much smaller than you.

6

Examining Your Puzzle

Putting together the pieces of your puzzle may bring you to the brink of seriously examining the picture they create. This can begin to unsettle you. If you have physical or emotional reactions to the recollections you have gathered, it is possible that you are an adult survivor of incest. Your interest in this book, for example, may be an indication that something incestually traumatic happened to you as a child.

Disturbing Feelings

At this point you may find it difficult to get past your fear of drawing conclusions about your possible abuse. Proceed carefully and slowly. Allow yourself time to digest sudden insights about your childhood, family, or adult experiences. (You may want to proceed to chapters 10 and 11 to read about choosing a therapist and learning to build your recovery support team.)

You must be aware that it may take some time for you to accept that in your early years, as an expression of your abuse, you masturbated excessively, sexually molested another child, or suffered nightmares. It can be hard to accept your childhood behaviors, especially, when they bring to mind your adult struggles to maintain and project stable profiles of yourself.

Sometimes, too, it is disturbing to realize that your parents may not have been as protective of you as you wish they had been. You can feel overwhelmingly sad to fully comprehend that they brought disappointment and hurt into your life.

Further, it is difficult to face your toxic adult coping behaviors. Acknowledging them is painful and arduous. Working to change them is even more so. Confronting your unknown self can be frightening.

Remember, though, that you cannot make the evidence of your possible abuse disappear simply by wishing it away. You've tried that since you were a child and it hasn't changed the way you feel about yourself. Therefore, it is helpful to pull together your insights *now*. It is extremely important to examine the possible circumstances that created your newly identified physical, mental, or behavioral symptoms.

Your List

Carol sought help initially because she was in emotional pain and unable to trace its cause. Like many adult survivors of incest, she was not consciously aware of her childhood molestation.

Carol and her therapist gathered Carol's puzzle pieces, or information, into a list. Using the words *triggers, childhood, family of origin, adult themes,* and *memories* as headings, they compiled a list that looked like this:

Triggers

- panic attacks
- became sober
- gaps in memories of childhood
- disturbed when standing next to elderly men

Childhood

- spent summers with grandparents
- mother worked nights as a nurse
- dad was on disability
- drew body parts in first grade
- skin rashes, from three to ten years old

- started drinking, thirteen years old
- read escape novels
- felt ashamed of self

Family of Origin

- family fought
- grandparents lived in the country
- grandfather drank
- grandmother was very religious
- children had to take care of parents
- was special to grandfather
- parents were always busy
- grandparents never took care of brothers
- was called a crybaby by family

Adult Themes

- alcoholic
- promiscuous
- workaholic
- low self-esteem
- passive in relationships

Memories

- recurring image of being fondled
- thinking about that image is difficult
- feel upset when someone talks about incest

As Carol and her therapist reviewed her list, several clues began to point to a theme of victimization.

The Clues

Carol's therapist knew that survivors suffer panic attacks. She also knew that Carol's early sexually explicit drawings were uncommon themes for children of that age. Carol said her parents were emotionally unavailable to her. Her dislike for a certain type of person indicated that at some point in her early life Carol may have been frightened by someone with a similar profile. Carol had large gaps in her memory about her youth, when she spent a great deal of time with her grandparents. That she developed a medically inexplicable rash also intrigued her therapist.

Carol's therapist was further alerted to the possibility of incest when Carol discussed her coping behavior and extreme discomfort in revealing her recurring image. Carol became very upset when her therapist suggested that she might be an adult survivor of incest. These clues led the therapist to conclude that Carol could indeed be an adult survivor of incest.

Affirming Conclusions

Carol was fortunate because she was able to identify a memory of being molested by way of her recurring image. Some survivors, however, remember nothing. How do they give themselves affirmation about their incest? For these people, memories frequently surface after they have been in treatment for a while, but in the meantime they are uncertain about trusting their intuition. One of the questions they ask most often is, "How do I know it happened when I can't pull together a specific experience?"

In their wonderful book *The Courage to Heal*,[1] Ellen Bass and Laura Davis comment that they rarely met an inquiring person who later found that she was not an adult survivor of incest. Many therapists agree that clear memories do not need to be evoked in order to work through the recovery process.

Admitting the Truth

Adults have difficulty facing their incest for much the same reasons they block the memories of their early experience. Addressing the reality can be overwhelming, because their projected fears of the problems that could develop if they seek further investigation or treatment are sometimes accurate.

While survivors can face what they were unable to confront

when they were children, fears of abandonment and death remain for adults and young children alike.

The fear of losing contact with family members and other loved ones sometimes becomes reality. When survivors confess their suspected abuse to loved ones, their loved ones, too, may be unable to accept the enormity of the information. To compensate for their feelings, family members or close friends may badger, ignore, or discontinue contact with survivors who have already suffered dreadfully.

An adult survivor whose partner walks the denial path himself may fear that he will withdraw from the relationship in retribution.

Children rarely make up incest stories. Adult survivors, likewise, do not invent their intuitive or painful feelings of shame and humiliation about an incest experience. These feelings are common in adult survivors. As one therapist remarked, "You can't make up your feelings. You either have them or you don't." Feelings are not quantifiable, but you know they are there.

You also know that you were born, but most people do not remember the experience. By all accounts, some births are pretty traumatic. Even though you have no recollection of a difficult experience, you trust that the event occurred as reported. The same argument holds true for those who have been molested. When all signs point to the fact of incest, that is basically all you need to know before delving more deeply.

Accepting Your Puzzle

Having completed your puzzle, you must decide whether you are ready to deal with your incest. Chapter 7 discusses the recovery process in detail, outlining important elements you should consider before committing yourself to the difficult task of making yourself feel better.

7

The Recovery Process:

Healing from Incest

Healing from an incest experience can be complicated and may take some time. The "scratch and dent" approach to treatment does not work. At times you will tire of thinking about your incest, and it will be natural for you to resist pursuing your recovery. *All incest survivors have these feelings.*

Recovering from incest may be likened to the healing process that takes place after a person suffers a great loss: certain step-by-step stages must occur in order for the bereaved—or the incest victim—to attain inner peace.

The Recovery Stages

The Emotionally Painful Stage

You are in a crisis that is caused by one of the triggers identified in chapter 1. You are in emotional or physical pain, or you have experienced a flashback or image. You cannot explain why this pain has suddenly emerged, but you realize that your desperate feelings must receive some attention.

The Confused Stage

You begin to draw together some of your incest pieces and suspect that something happened to you in your earlier life, but you cannot remember what it was. You dig further and are confused by surfacing memories or realizations about your family and yourself. You may experience anxiety attacks or pockets of craziness at times. You could be committed to your therapy, but are not convinced that you are an adult survivor. As a matter of fact, thinking about your possible incest is very unsettling.

The Denial Stage

"Wait a minute," you think. You are having difficulty digesting your emerging truth, because you believe it will only create more pain or that you are one of those very special people who can handle your incest without help. You want to believe that you made up your thoughts, memories, or feelings.

Acknowledging the Shame Stage

You begin to realize that denying your abuse does not alleviate your fears or pain. Instead, you become more aware of your shameful feelings. You recognize that they have kept you from fully expressing your anger to the person or persons who hurt you and sustained your guilt feelings about the experience.

The Anger Stage

You begin to express your anger toward the appropriate people. You may be angry with your close parent or parents for not protecting you. It is a surprising and pleasant sensation to vent your anger, and you feel some personal empowerment. But then you remember that exercising your personal power when you were a child caused your caretakers to abandon you emotionally. To be strong meant to be alone, which frightens you.

The Gatekeeper Stage

You become frightened by your anger because it frightened your vulnerable inner child. Your survival coping defenses are fighting to protect your inner child. You may reexperience your anxiety or panic attacks.

This is your opportunity to confront your gatekeepers by befriending them and acknowledging that they have served you well. You begin to understand that you have the ability to invite them into your life rather than being led by them. You recognize that they are feelings, not orders for you to react in your old predictable ways.

The Sadness and Letting Go Stage

As you integrate your new feelings and beliefs into your life, you begin to experience trust. You feel safer to be who you are with your support team, and this means that you can freely express your sadness over the loss of your inner child's innocence. You now know that your abuse will not make you crazy. Your moments of anxiety are further apart and less intense. You are free to follow your newfound belief in yourself.

The Integration Stage

You have had the opportunity to practice your new behavior and feel confident with your own perceptions of life, though they may differ from those of others. This stage occurs when you have purged yourself of fear, anger, and sadness. The reality of incest is part of you, but not apart from you. You may, in time, forgive your abuser, but remember that this is not necessary for you to be able to work through your recovery process.

As you go through these stages, you may confront your abuser or other family members, reach out, for the first time, to safe people for support, begin to express your desires without feeling guilty, or discover the power of pursuing assistance through a spiritual source. Most important, you begin to love yourself.

No Predictable Pattern

The recovery stages do not always follow the predictable path outlined in the previous paragraphs. As a matter of fact, you may become exhausted during recovery as you experience a roller coaster of emotions. You may feel anger one moment, only to experience joy the next.

It is normal to question whether it is possible to feel love and anger toward your abuser. You may become much more upset with your nonoffending parent or parents. It is difficult to come to terms with the fact that you were unprotected by those who were supposed to be the most nurturing.

The stages often repeat themselves. For example, you may feel you have resolved your feelings about a particular incest experience, only to remember another one by the same person or others. This leads to a recycling of your recovery process.

Stress and Exhaustion

The recovery process generates stress and exhaustion, occasionally leaving you feeling as though you have been through the wringer of an old-fashioned washing machine. One survivor said, "If I didn't have a sense of humor, I think I would be in really big trouble. I have experienced dozens of panic attacks. But luckily, they occur further apart these days. I wouldn't wish this on anyone, except, of course, my abuser!"

The healing process can take months or years, depending on a survivor's commitment, personal recovery timing, and support systems. Because life does not stand still for anyone, people are sometimes forced to halt recovery while tending to a sick relative or recuperating from a major operation or move. Recognizing that no time is a good time to walk through a fire, it is helpful to assess whether you are ready to make the commitment to walking the recovery path.

Healing Takes Time

As you begin to heal, you must allow yourself to flow with the process. In other words, do not put yourself under pressure by telling yourself that you must complete the recovery stages within a certain time frame. Many survivors become discouraged because they have no control over the time it takes for their sadness to dissipate. The healing process involves the ability to let go of your need to be in emotional control of yourself twenty-four hours a day. Are you prepared to trust the process?

You may find that you embark on the healing process several times before you actually make a commitment to doing the soul-searching required by the work. It is okay to put your healing on hold if your life is sustaining a degree of harmony and balance. Take care, however, not to postpone the inevitable by believing that your times of high emotional pain will mysteriously subside if you ignore them.

Is It Time to Begin Recovery Work?

Considering that good treatment is not painless and that people do not feel better until they have faced themselves honestly, it is safe to assume that you may wish to postpone your recovery work indefinitely. But the fact remains that your problems do not go away unless you deal with them.

With that in mind, take this opportunity to assess how harmonious your life appears to you currently and what you are willing to do to effect a permanent change of your self-destructive habits and improve your sense of personal worth.

8

Decision Time:

Are You Ready for Incest Recovery Work?

Now that you have had the opportunity to examine your incest puzzle and reach some conclusions, you may either want to deny your childhood abuse or commit to working toward recovery as an adult survivor of incest.

It is helpful to remember that many adult survivors of incest deny their experiences. Denial is one of those gatekeepers or defense mechanisms that protects the inner child. It is normal and subsides over time.

Expressions of Denial

Some survivors, although acknowledging that they were abused, deny that the abuse affects them. They may be pained by such behaviors as recurring poor relationships, severe mood swings, or compulsive spending, but they refuse to believe that incest could be at the root of their problems.

Thus, survivors frequently rationalize their abuse. The following are familiar comments they offer.

Tina

Okay, so maybe I am an adult survivor. What do you want me to do about it?

Carolyn

How do I know that looking any further into my abuse will make me feel better?

Mike

Look, this happened long ago. I now realize it happened, but I really don't think it had anything to do with my drug addiction.

Diane

It's life. Everyone has something bad happen to them. I wouldn't be a very strong person if I let my incest experience affect me.

Sherree

I don't know that I want to work any harder. It seems to me that I'll only feel worse if I think about it any more.

Dan

I love my father and I'm not going to jeopardize our relationship by talking about his abuse of me. It's my mother I really have problems with.

Kim

How in the world would anyone believe that I was molested by my mother? Talk about freaking people out. I'm not thought well of now, as it is.

~

All these statements were made by people who initially resisted probing any further into their early experiences. Perhaps you have felt like them. They were frightened by their feelings and worried that they would face rejection from others if they pursued their recovery. This may also be true for you.

When you review the incest recovery process and determine the value of a balance of harmony in your present life, it is helpful to assume that you will question your decision to get better. You may think to yourself, "This is more than I want to deal with," or "Is it worth the pain I'll experience?"

The Circle of Balance or Harmony

Native American cultures encourage inner balance by stressing the importance of six fundamental areas. They understand that physical well-being, spiritual well-being, relaxation, work, balanced emotions, and healthy relationships are essential to inner harmony. The Hawaiians, for example, refer to this harmony as *lokahi.*

As you review the merits of committing to the healing process, consider how your life has reflected harmony and balance. When people review these areas of well-being, they may realize that they have never learned to live a well-rounded life. Consequently, they conclude that spending time reviewing their living habits would help them feel more whole. Some survivors, for example, after examining their areas of well-being, acknowledge that they have neglected their bodies. Or in reviewing their relationships they become keenly aware that they have difficulty sustaining satisfying intimacy for fear of being left alone.

Take a moment to consider what you do to experience greater harmony in your personal life. Do you think it is worth your while to spend time to evaluate how you are faring physically, spiritually, in relationships, in "play" time, and work, as well as emotionally? If you do, write down what you do to satisfy yourself in these areas. Keep in mind that in dealing with your incest, you will be freer to lead a more balanced life.

Adult survivors of incest seldom take time to question themselves about what they want and need in order to be happy. One man said, "I never paid attention to what I wanted, because no one ever listened to me anyway."

Now is your opportunity to focus on your wants and needs. As you probably are aware, you will be asked by your therapist—and later by others—to look within yourself for those answers. After you have reviewed the balance (or lack of balance) in your life, you may be more motivated to begin your recovery work.

Your Strengths

Before you decide to undertake recovery work, it also is helpful to evaluate your personal strengths. That is, you acquired many positive coping styles for surviving your early trauma. Identifying and drawing on those personal strengths will get you through the rough recovery times. It is important to remember this.

One survivor, during periods of high anxiety, comforted herself by taking hot baths to help her relax. This was an identifiable strength. Another survivor, after shedding her tears, used her sense of humor to reframe her pain. Yet another survivor wrote beautiful poetry to express her feelings. Still another told herself that since she had been able, to that point, to survive her father's betrayal, she could learn to love herself. All those people exhibited strong and positive qualities, which were assets to their recovery.

Take some time to write down your strengths. *You have them.* They may include such traits as the following:

- I am a good listener.
- I usually keep my commitments.
- I am loyal.
- I have a good sense of humor.
- People can depend on me.
- I enjoy a hobby.
- I allow myself to cry.
- I never stop trying.
- I like the way I look.
- I am a responsible parent.
- I protect my children.

- I love animals.
- I care about the environment.
- I take good care of my body.

A Word About Addiction

If you have an addiction with which you have not dealt, it is best to work toward stabilizing that problem before tackling the incest recovery work. Dealing with addiction first will build the foundation for your later healing from your childhood molestation. Do not attempt to work on both issues at once. Many people who have attempted to do so have become overwhelmed and returned to substance abuse.

Further Confirmation

If you still wonder whether entering an incest recovery program would be best for you, the questions and answers in the next chapter should help you resolve your doubts and make up your mind to do so.

9

Questions from Adult Survivors of Incest

Adult survivors of incest who examine their puzzle understandably have questions. As you have reviewed the information in this book, you may have found that you share some of the same concerns.

The questions most frequently asked by survivors have to do with their certainty about having been abused and their worries about their vulnerability during recovery. This chapter addresses these valid concerns.

~

How can I be sure that I am a survivor of incest?

This is a good question. Short of having a camera in the room during the time of the assault, no one can be absolutely sure she was molested—unless she remembers its occurrence. Even recall can be distorted, so it is important to examine all the puzzle pieces closely.

As you examined your clues, you may have discovered some themes. While many of your pieces of evidence may be similar to the symptoms shared by other trauma survivors, there is a difference.

First, you began to feel intuitively that you were molested by someone you trusted, and second, you experienced some panic or moments of high anxiety as you delved more deeply into your puzzle—moments termed "pockets of craziness." Having these feelings awaken the feeling that perhaps your life was physically threatened during some period in your childhood. If you cannot relate them to an accident or other catastrophe, they could be related to an incest experience.

It is important to remember that you do not need a court of law to affirm your truth. Examining the possibility that you are a survivor is the first step in the healing process of post-traumatic stress disorder, the syndrome described in chapter 5.

The process of looking into a suspected abuse more than likely gave you the information you need to come to some conclusions. It also put you on the road to gaining personal insight, a goal of any type of therapeutic intervention. In other words, you have nothing to lose by exploring the possibility of an incest experience.

Furthermore, if you do conclude that you are an adult survivor of incest, you have options as to how to pursue resolution of your early trauma. For example, it is not necessary that you confront your abuser physically while you are in recovery. Many people fear that this is a requirement. Even though it is not an option for some people, they refuse to probe into their past because of their fear of having to face their molester. There are many ways to confront the assault without your abuser being present.

Adult survivors of incest have difficulty trusting their feelings. The process of recovering from incest assists people to gain confidence about affirming their truth. Your consideration of your puzzle pieces can give you important personal validation.

~

Will working through my incest cause me to become crazy?

When you are responsibly guided through your recovery, the chances that you will become "crazy" or lose touch with reality are slim. Almost every adult survivor of incest has felt crazy at one point or another in her recovery, but she was not insane. It is normal to feel that things are getting out of control when, after many years of being suppressed, your emotions come out of hiding.

Repressed rage occasionally threatens to overwhelm survivors. Their anger can frighten them, especially if they have never been able to express themselves in healthy ways. The anger subsides over time as the survivor expresses herself and learns effective skills for coping with it. But during recovery, these feelings tend to present themselves in ways that make people feel they are losing their minds.

Your recovery support team (see chapter 11) will help you during rough times. Your therapist will be your main reality check or anchor. You will learn to accept the fact that you will sometimes feel uncomfortable. Unfortunately, growth is not painless.

Outpatient therapy can help you feel safe and secure. If you do not feel that it provides enough support, you can always ask your therapist about inpatient facilities. And remember that you can also spend time with loved ones.

You have the choice to get all the support you feel you need. The supply is inexhaustible. Too many people have been taught not to ask for support and therefore expect rejection.

Working through the recovery process will probably not make you crazy. Instead, it will give you a healthier outlook on life.

~

Can I really change my self-destructive ways of dealing with problems?

You certainly can! Although it is never easy and no one can do the work for you, you have the capacity within yourself to make healthy changes in your life.

Should you conclude that you are an adult survivor of incest, you will need to make a commitment to the recovery process, which includes therapy. You will find that working through an early incest experience is difficult at best. Although the end results can be wonderful, the process of recovery is not.

A commitment to any brave undertaking is difficult to make and to keep. So you may find it helpful to remind yourself daily why you want to change and to grow. The reasons most people do not explore their past is that they do not wish to reexperience some of their former painful times.

It is important to remember that you are not living your trauma now. And self-exploration always presents challenges. It is also important to consider that you may fall back into old self-destructive habits during your recovery. This is to be expected. It is good, however, to discuss and examine how the habits reemerged and to climb back "on the wagon." Know that you are not perfect and that it takes a lot of practice to learn something new, like a healthy style of living.

Mental health experts often feel that adult survivors of incest make exciting clients. This is because survivors are intensely committed to pursuing mental peace. The changes they make can be extraordinary. They may be difficult to make, but they are always impressive.

~

I have heard incest survivors speak about their inner child. What does this mean as it relates to incest?

Your inner child is the little girl who was emotionally damaged during violation. Although children can be hurt physically, the inner child usually refers to that part of you that suffered abuse and then denied her emotional pain.

You may not have been aware of her presence for the same reasons you could not remember your incest. When you begin to reflect on your past, you will probably not wish to acknowledge this childlike and vulnerable part of yourself. In fact, when you recall yourself as a young child you may think of yourself as bad, spoiled, worried, cranky, sad, forlorn, or unlovable.

As an adult you have more than likely felt very young and vulnerable during moments of stress. This is usual for anyone; however, most survivors are somewhat overtaken by their inner-child feelings during these times. Adult survivors of incest have a difficult time accepting that their inner child can have a great deal of control over their emotions.

Intellectually you, too, may think that you should not feel childlike because this causes you to feel weak or powerless. Consequently, you deny that needy, dependent part of yourself, the part that never received the nurturance it deserved. If you are a parent yourself, you can understand why your own children may have a tantrum when they feel neglected. This tactic is quite similar to the survivor's inner-child attempts to gain attention for that long-ago pain. Just as bodies reflect nutritional neglect, so too do spirits reflect emotional negligence.

Your therapist will help you to become acquainted with your inner child. While you begin to know yourself in this manner, you may find that you really were very lovable. You will grieve over your hurt and nurture your old pain. You will embrace your inner child and accept her for who she is. As you accept her, you will begin to accept yourself. You will come to know that you and she are the same person.

After a while you will enjoy your inner child. You will also learn to incorporate her appropriately into your life. And when you struggle with her for control of your emotions, you will gently take the lead. You will know when you need to be the responsible adult and when you can allow your playfulness to emerge.

The inner child is not exclusively identified with adult survivors of incest. It is also an important part of any self-examination after one has experienced childhood trauma, such as growing up with alcoholic parents.

The inner child is excluded from consciousness by people whose emotional growing process was obstructed because they were unable to develop normally. Anyone who was raised in a nonfunctioning or dysfunctional home is susceptible to suppressing her inner child. Surprisingly, a great many people have never acknowledged their childhood pain and continue to ignore a very important part of themselves.

Getting Help

Adding these answers to all the other information you have found in this book, you should be ready to make an affirmative decision to walk the recovery path. It is extremely important to put together your support recovery team before embarking on your healing. Few people are able to walk through this process alone. You must have people who support you when you are upset and believe you when you speak your truth.

After taking time to assess and appreciate your strengths once more, consider what you need in the way of support from others. Chapters 10 and 11 tell you how to assemble the safe people to assist you on your journey to serenity.

10

Choosing Your Therapist

It is invaluable to work with a professional who specializes in sexual trauma. Establishing a therapeutic relationship with such a guide gives you the opportunity to express your unresolved feelings and practice trusting another person. Your therapist is one of the most important helpers in your recovery, so choose that person wisely.

Before arranging an initial interview with a professional, ask others who have been in treatment whom they would recommend. Members of self-help groups and human service agencies may be able to suggest qualified practitioners.

National resource groups include Adult Children of Alcoholics, Survivors of Incest Anonymous, and Alcoholics Anonymous. Mental health association and center staff can provide referrals. You may also request names from your community's rape or domestic violence programs. Other professionals—ministers, law enforcement officers, or doctors—can give you suggestions.

Give some thought to whether you would feel comfortable working with a therapist of the opposite sex. Ask yourself what you want to gain from your treatment, and be willing to allocate time and money toward your recovery. Remember, your emotional and physical well-being are at stake. Most of all, keep in mind what you need for yourself at this time.

You have a right to expect that your therapist has the following essential qualifications.

Knowledge of Incest

Adult survivor of incest recovery work is a specialized area of expertise. Your therapist should understand the stages of recovery and the therapeutic techniques that have been proven useful. Your therapist should be a certified or licensed practitioner in addition to having received training in sexual assault treatment.

These experts can be found in a variety of mental health disciplines. You could select for your therapist a psychiatrist (a trained medical doctor), a psychologist (licensed in mental health testing), a marriage and family therapist, a clinical social worker, or other licensed mental health professional.

It is helpful to have a therapist who has published articles or books on surviving incest. Your therapist should be able to identify other experts and be well read with regard to current sexual assault literature. As a responsible professional, she (or he) should be a member of a national professional organization such as the American Association of Marriage and Family Therapists or the American Psychological Association.

Compatible Therapeutic Style

You need to find a therapist who suits your personality. While any good therapist is caring and understanding, some are more direct or open with their comments or suggestions. Others listen and volunteer remarks only occasionally. Their styles simply represent differing approaches to their work. Try to determine which style reaches you most effectively.

Open-mindedness

Whatever style your therapist assumes, he (or she) should be open-minded and accept your truth and experience without being judgmental. Working toward recovery of adult survivors of incest is a relatively new discipline, so therapists must remain open to new approaches that may benefit their clients. Select a therapist who is responsive to your questions and flexible in her thinking.

Commitment

The therapist you choose should be prepared to work with you over a long period of time. She must be willing to respond to you at inconvenient times if necessary and give you ample notice should she move or otherwise be unavailable. To put it another way, your therapist must be considerate and consistent.

Responsibility

However, your therapist must not assume responsibility for you. She must be able to establish and be a role model of healthy boundaries. She should consistently push you to look within yourself for the answers to your questions.

~

Be honest with your therapist. You may have a tendency to minimize your incest and its effect on you, so be sure to volunteer as much information about yourself as you can. Try not to assume that your therapist is labeling you.

If you can afford it while considering whom to choose, visit a therapist a second time if you feel your initial session was unsatisfactory. You may have projected some of your own feelings onto her because you were nervous.

Try to maintain an open mind during treatment. Your therapist may ask you to complete a written exercise or perform some other unfamiliar activity. Allow yourself the opportunity to experience new feelings and share them with your helper.

Most important of all, give yourself permission to trust your therapist to be your guide.

11

Your Recovery Support Team

Recovering from your early incest experience presents a great challenge. Alice, a wonderfully courageous adult survivor, put it this way: "I have often felt like a battlefield, marched over by two armies. One army is marching to allow my inner child to share her truth, and the gatekeepers are marching to protect her from the truth. Sometimes all I want is a truce. I just want the war to be over. Speed it up, or slow it down, but get some relief here."

Because the survivor's internal struggle is so intense, you will require a support team to help you face your battles in recovery. Just as you would not attempt to climb a mountain without the necessary supplies or strategies, you need to have at least one person, and preferably several, who can be your reality check during this process. Your support team serves as your anchor during both your high-anxiety moments and your calmer, more reflective times.

Anchors

As an adult survivor of incest, you cannot fully recover from your abuse without the aid of someone who or something that serves to ground you in the "here and now." Your anchors remind you of who you are while you are allowing your conflicts to unfold and resolve themselves.

Your anchors form your recovery support team. As in sports teams, it may include one or more coaches, as well as teammates who have played your position or complement you in some way. Your support team acknowledges your pain and validates your truth. It must be safe.

Choosing Safe Members

It is vitally important to assure that those whom you assemble to support you during your most vulnerable moments are fully qualified to do so. The feelings of shame that you have begun to recognize may cause you embarrassment. You may still feel a sense of responsibility for your incest. You may also fear that sharing your experience will alienate others or cause them to believe that you are crazy.

You must understand that disclosing your incest experience is a special gift to be bestowed only on those who are worthy. Yet being worthy has nothing to do with one person's being superior to someone whose help you do not request. The criterion is simply that any support team member must be able to under-stand your pain, encourage your strengths, validate that you were *not* responsible for your childhood experience, and honor your anonymity. Some people you like and admire may be un-able to deal with your experience and therefore would be unsuit-able candidates for your purpose. You must give yourself permission to select your helpers carefully.

Who Is Safe?

In putting together your support team, consider what you re-quire to help you feel safe. How do you want others to assist you?

Here are some questions you may want to ask yourself.

- Do I want to be able to cry in the presence of my team members?
- Do I need a guide who understands the recovery process and assists me in confronting my fears?

- Do I need to feel free to phone my helpers during inconvenient periods of the day or night?
- Do I want nurturing?
- Do I want someone to reassure me that my difficult emotional times will pass?
- Do I need the help of a professional guide, someone who understands how to use her training to enhance my recovery?
- Do I want someone of the opposite sex on my team?
- Do I want helpers who can understand when I simply want to take a break from my recovery work?
- Do I feel that I am open to asking others for help?
- Am I willing to acknowledge that my team members may not always be available to help me?

Now think about someone you already know who is trustworthy. Think, too, about anyone you have recently met who may be willing to become a supporter, someone who, after initial conversations, appears to have successfully resolved her own problems.

Here are some additional questions you may wish to consider.

- Would any of my family members understand and support me?
- Is there anyone in any of my school classes, church, or clubs to whom I can particularly relate?
- Which of my friends would empathize if I discussed my incest?
- Do I know anyone who has been through a similar experience?
- Who of my family, friends, or acquaintances can refer me to a therapist who specializes in working with adult survivors of incest?
- What groups are available for someone with my concerns?
- Who of the people I know would not be able to understand my incest recovery work?
- Whom do I know who would not be frightened if I expressed my anger?

You may be fortunate to know several people who can be on

your support team, but for the most part adult survivors of incest begin with one or two safe sources. They build upon their team as they join support groups and attend adult survivor of incest workshops or seminars.

Remember that you can be strongly influenced by others when you are feeling vulnerable. So keep in mind that it can be most helpful to associate with people who have a positive attitude. People who have experienced trauma and have worked through their problems in a productive manner can be compassionate without becoming totally involved with your pain. You have probably known them. They have been a schoolteacher, counselor, working associate, minister, or close friend. By studying their lives, you have an opportunity to emulate their successful behavior.

You may also wish to use your team members selectively. In other words, some people are better at consoling than being playful. Others may not know anything about incest, yet are available to listen to you, to accept you, to sympathize. Each of your team members can bring a special gift to you as you proceed through your recovery. Value their usefulness.

Introducing Your Incest

When you disclose your abuse to others and request their support, you are taking a chance. You risk the rejection you knew so well as a child. Although you recognize that you are now an adult, you may also feel childlike and frightened, which is normal. Do not let that stop you from asking for help. When you approach the topic with a potential member you may want to phrase your words in any number of ways. For example:

> You know, Amy, it is very difficult for me to tell you this
> because I feel frightened, but I would like to share with
> you my secret that I was molested as a child.
> Ron, I have been thinking about pulling together a group of
> people who can support me as I get involved in my
> recovery work from an early incest experience. Would you
> consider being one of those people?
> I've always been a private person, but I realize I will need

some assistance now from supportive folks. Janet, would
you think about becoming a support person for me as I
look more deeply into my incest experience?

I am happy to be able to ask for your help. Please consider
supporting me through my incest recovery process.

I value you and feel comfortable with you. Do you think I
could call on you sometimes as I work through my incest
recovery?

You may be pleasantly surprised to find that most of those
you have asked to help will respond positively. However, if you
sense that someone is becoming frightened or drawing away
because of your request, remember that there is nothing wrong
with you. She or he is not ready to be helpful. That is the
person's choice and certainly no reflection upon you.

Most people are willing to help others. They may be confused
about your problem, but they serve you by listening. Others have
been through a similar experience and you intuitively feel their
understanding.

You will find that your team members can be drawn from a
variety of backgrounds, and they may be people from whom you
would not at first expect to receive help. One survivor gained a
great deal of strength from a male friend with whom she had
established a platonic relationship during her recovery. He was
willing to act as a role model of healthy male behavior. Her
father had been her molester, and she learned through her friend
that men can be loving without being manipulating.

Another survivor found that she grew close to a woman in a
support group who was very different from her. The first survivor was lesbian and involved in many human rights issues; the
second was married and saw herself as a homemaker. Maintain
an open mind as you choose team members.

Your Spirituality

While you must have compassionate people on your recovery
support team, you may find it helpful to consider that another
source from which to draw strength is a belief in a higher
power. A higher power can be God, nature, or some other

source of energy to sustain you during troubled times. This essence or force may strengthen you in ways that cannot be measured or calculated. It calms you and brings you peace after you have been through a battle of inner turmoil. People pray, write, or meditate in order to make contact with their silent comforter. Most who seek inner strength eventually allow their spirituality to assist them in their recovery work.

Strength in Support

Knowing that you do not have to face your fears without a backup group can be reassuring. Your support team is your fan club. You have to walk your recovery path alone, but it does not hurt to know that others will be proud of you at the end of your journey.

Chapter 12 provides information on additional recovery tools or anchors that have helped adult survivors of incest.

Other Recovery Tools

When you were a child and caught a cold, you probably enjoyed being cared for. Hot chicken soup, clean sheets, and aspirin made the illness easier to bear. Similarly, your support team or anchors, as well as other resources, can make your painful emotional times easier to endure as you progress through your incest recovery. They are necessary to keep you feeling grounded in the present.

Adult survivors of incest describe various ways of feeling comforted. These anchors fall into four categories of activity—insightful, playful, physical, and self-nurturing.

None of these can replace your "people" anchors—your therapist and other support team members, whom you can meet at a variety of support groups, in a class, and through other friends and family members. Your tendency as a survivor may be to over-involve or isolate yourself so that you cannot find time to discuss your problem. As you know, it is important that you unburden yourself and share your secret with safe people.

But there are other ways to receive support as you experience your recovery stages. Some anchors help you obtain insight, while others engage your thoughts without engaging your emotions. Many help you to feel grounded and centered. They can assist you in clarifying your thoughts and becoming detached from your earlier abuse.

As you approach your recovery work, list some of the activities that bring you pleasure and peace of mind. Later you can add to your list—or find that you already use—some of the recovery tools or anchors suggested here.

Insight-oriented Anchors

Activities that encourage you to face your past while practicing new behavior or thinking are most helpful. The book *The Courage To Heal*[1] suggests written exercises that, when shared with another survivor, draw out your repressed feelings. Writing is one example of an insight-oriented activity that serves as a tool in your recovery work. Some helpful exercises include writing

- your strengths in a daily journal
- a letter to your abuser
- a letter to your inner child
- a wish list
- your autobiography
- your support team members' names
- a letter to your nonoffending parent or parents
- what you remember of your molestation
- letters of encouragement to yourself

It is a good idea to share your writing with a safe person on your support team. Sharing your written material also gives you an opportunity to receive active support and validation. Finding that you are not rejected because of what you have written helps you to gain more confidence in yourself. It is extraordinarily important for you to *experience* acceptance.

The following provide additional routes to gaining understanding about your abuse.

Visualization or Meditation

When your mind relaxes you have an opportunity to create a picture or image, which can be particularly helpful if it is one in which you envision yourself feeling better. For example, you may see yourself looking radiantly healthy and laughing with one of your friends. Or you may envision yourself in a peaceful, beautiful place. You can also project your picture into the future and envision yourself doing things that make you feel good about yourself.

Some survivors envision themselves as children and later imagine themselves reassuring their inner child. This helps them to face and overcome their childhood fears and experiences. Eventually, they merge their inner child vision with their adult vision of themselves, which helps them to feel whole.

Meditation is a technique for relaxing the mind. With practice, you can sit in a state of calm without thinking about anything. What you experience is a clear, peaceful feeling without the interruption of "monkey mind" (racing thoughts). Meditation offers you a good opportunity to rest without falling asleep.

Hypnosis

Brian Weiss, a psychiatrist who uses hypnosis in his work with adults who have been molested and author of the book *Many Lives, Many Masters*,[2] describes hypnosis as focused concentration. Another psychiatrist, Sal Fusaro of Miami, Florida, describes hypnosis as an altered state of consciousness in which the logical mind is turned off so that it accesses metaphorical or symbolic thinking.

Hypnosis is a tool employed by therapists with adult survivors of incest. Neither sleep in the conventional sense nor in any way a controlling technique, it is used to assist survivors in recalling their abuse.

People in trance block outside interferences so that they can focus on remembering or receiving positive reinforcement. They never do anything under hypnosis that is inconsistent with their moral or ethical values. It is a state of deep relaxation in which they are able to feel calm and safe.

Hypnosis has been an extremely effective resource for adult survivors of incest who wish to enhance their memory. However, should you wish to experience this technique, be sure to consult a qualified professional; it is almost impossible to have a productive session unless you have complete faith in the therapist.

Audiotapes

Wonderful tapes are available to help people overcome habits and fears. They may contain soothing sounds or messages of positive thinking.

One way to gain insight into yourself is to record yourself speaking about your concerns. You may wish to tape yourself reciting a therapeutic story or substitute this exercise for writing in a journal. Make a tape and share it with a friend if you feel uncomfortable discussing your thoughts in person.

Revisiting Special Places

When you feel strong enough to confront some of your fears, you may wish to return to your childhood town or house. You need the cooperation of your support team for this exercise. It is important to remember that returning to former haunts where you were abused can resurrect bad feelings. So check with your therapist to okay your visit and have a team member accompany you. Returning to the "scene of the crime" can be very powerful and healing, but it must be done at the right time. If you overwhelm yourself too soon into your recovery, you will not want to continue with your healing work.

Reviewing Family Pictures

This exercise is most helpful when you share it with a friend. It gives you an opportunity to appreciate yourself as a child and consider each family member from an adult perspective. You can describe the pictures and share feelings about how you perceived your role in your family.

This is a wonderful way for you to realize that you could do nothing to prevent your sexual abuse because you have direct pictorial evidence that you were a vulnerable child when your molestation occurred. As you examine your pictures you may realize that there is and was nothing shameful about you.

Rituals

Ceremonies are helpful because they can symbolically represent resolution of your past. One survivor pulled together articles that represented her childhood pain and, accompanied by a friend, burned them along a riverbank. Another invited friends to a party, asking them to bring something that represented strength.

Some of the gifts included a stuffed bear, a smooth stone, and a magic wand. She referred to them throughout her recovery. Such rituals, which have existed for centuries, can be a positive factor in healing and growth.

Books

There are many books on incest, including personal stories written by adult survivors of incest, comprehensive texts describing the recovery process, self-help guides, and workbooks. Choose those books which speak to your individual pain. You may also find helpful information from books on healing, for example, *The Other Side of the Family, Scream Louder*, and *The Twelve Steps to Self-Parenting*.[3]

Insight-oriented activities serve to assist you in experiencing the reality of your abuse and remind you of your strengths. They should not be undertaken as though you were going to a grocery store and checking off your list of items to buy. Instead, they need to be considered and attended to when you have time to process the information that they access. You can become bombarded by your emotions if you attempt to elicit your feelings and awareness too quickly. Go slowly and be guided by your therapist.

Play Anchors

Adult survivors of incest have to learn to indulge in healthy play. Children who are molested often fail to learn how to have fun. Recovery should not be all work and no play. Adult survivor of incest workshops frequently spend time on play activities, which can be enjoyable experiences. You may wish to try some of those listed here.

Choose the types of play that pique your interest and ask your team members to participate with you. If you feel embarrassed the first time you attempt to do something playful, remember that it takes practice to ride a bicycle. You'll probably feel uncomfortable in the beginning, but don't worry. Doing anything for the first time feels strange.

Humor

A joke a day keeps the doctor away. This is true, because laughter can really be good medicine. Kind humor is a good defense mechanism, one that can also reframe your pain. If you know anyone who is especially humorous, ask her to go to dinner or participate in some other activity. Watch television comedies or Saturday morning cartoons. Read a funny novel. Laughter can relieve tension—and strengthen stomach muscles at the same time.

Roller-skating

This is a wonderful activity you can enjoy with a group of people. If you feel embarrassed, borrow a child for an afternoon or evening. You won't feel so conspicuous out on the rink and you will still have a great time.

Dancing

Go dancing with a platonic friend or arrange to meet people at a dance club after work. Put on your favorite dance music at home and allow your body to express itself. While you are dancing, remind yourself that you are wonderful.

Watch children dancing and observe how free they become. If you have small children, you will find that they are usually delighted to have you participate with them.

Music

Play your favorite music while driving your car or making dinner. Pretend you are the singer or the conductor of the orchestra. Allow yourself to sing loudly. Sing while you are in the shower and let yourself enjoy the sounds echoing against the walls. Play recorded musical comedies and imagine yourself as one of the cast members. Choose music you remember from your happiest moments—a high school prom or college party—and play it loudly.

Slumber Party

Invite your friends to your place for a slumber party. Rent a really bad horror movie, eat junk food, do one another's nails.

Finger-paint

Buy finger paints and spend some time getting messy with them. Use up sheets of paper and get paint on your nose.

Video Games

Rent a few video games or visit a video game arcade. Invite a friend to be your guest, take along five dollars in quarters, and play until your money runs out.

Amusement Parks

Spend a day at an amusement park and try out at least four rides. Get your fortune told and eat cotton candy. Take a child or two to a circus or spend time at a zoo.

Mindless Books

Read books that were forbidden to you as a child. Allow yourself to sample escape literature like romance novels or adventure stories.

Ball Games

Go to sports events and give yourself permission to cheer or yell at the players. Don't forget to buy at least one souvenir.

Sports

Join a volleyball or baseball team. Participate fully by coaching other members or sliding into third base.

~

Play is an important part of living. It disengages the mind and permits you to express the needs of your inner child in a healthy fashion. When you find yourself smiling during the activity, you know you are beginning to learn how to play.

Physical Anchors

Your body is a wonderful instrument. But, understandably, survivors often view it as a liability rather than an asset. Spend time reviewing your appearance in a mirror. Take time to appreciate your eyes, hair, nose, cheekbones, torso, and limbs. Value your attractiveness and look past your flaws. Everyone has them.

If you are ashamed of your appearance, remember that your body is not responsible for your feeling. Your body did not create your abuse; someone chose to abuse it. Your body is not an enemy. Your physical form can become one of your anchors. As you grow through recovery, your body will reflect your new health.

Exercise is an extension of your body or physical anchor. It stimulates energy and gives you a sense of well-being when done in moderation. There are many forms of exercise. Here are some examples.

Yoga

This system of disciplined exercises developed from the Hindu religion. Widely taught, the exercises involve deep breathing, stretching, and concentration.

Aerobics

This popular system of physical conditioning is designed to improve respiratory and circulatory functions through exercises that increase oxygen consumption. The energetic routines, accompanied by dance music, help to promote a positive attitude.

Walking

Also an aerobic exercise, walking is a great way to appreciate the outdoors while increasing blood flow through your body. And it costs nothing!

Water Sports

Another form of aerobics, swimming for exercise does not necessarily involve doing laps in a pool. Snorkeling, scuba diving, and water skiing are fun ways to enjoy the water and work your body.

Cycling

Still another aerobic exercise, cycling is one more excellent way to enjoy being outdoors and build stamina. Cycling clubs, which have emerged in recent years, give people an opportunity to meet and socialize.

Boxing

Working out anger on a punching bag can be very healing as well as physically good for you. A hobby limited in the past to males, boxing is becoming increasingly popular with women.

Cleaning

Many frustrated people have worked through their anger by scrubbing floors or scouring sinks. Aggressively sweeping floors is one way to accomplish two goals at once. Again, exercise need not cost a thing.

Construction Work

Building bookshelves, painting rooms, or wallpapering is another good way to exercise and help you feel good about yourself. One survivor enjoyed sawing the wood for her living room moldings.

Chopping Firewood

Another way to release energy, chopping firewood expends energy and accomplishes a goal.

~

It is important that you become newly acquainted with your body by treating it with respect and love. It will prove to be a wonderful anchor.

Self-nurturing Anchors

Adult survivors of incest have difficulty nurturing themselves. They may take great care of others, but when it comes to self-nurturing they can get stuck. Here are some wonderful ways for you to begin nurturing yourself.

Bathing

Taking a long, hot bubble bath is an inexpensive way to soothe your nerves when you have begun to feel consumed by your recovery work. Take care during your bath to appreciate your appearance. Read or daydream while you are in the tub, then use after-bath talc or lotion.

Comfort Foods

This self-nurturing exercise should not be confused with bingeing or any other eating disorder. Rather, comfort foods focus on nurturing yourself in a healthy way. For example, some people choose to have hot chocolate and toast when they feel sad. Others eat a home-cooked meal. One survivor enjoyed treating herself to hot buttered popcorn. Another made soup. One person nurtured herself by eating mashed potatoes and gravy. Comfort foods represent warmth and kindness. You need to treat yourself with that type of respect. You certainly would not pour salt on a wound; you would clean it and nourish it with medicine. Comfort food is the right type of medicine for your wound.

Stuffed Animals

When you do not have a sleeping partner, stuffed animals can provide you nighttime comfort. They can also be battered about when you want to express your anger. Many adults continue to sleep with a favorite stuffed toy.

Gardening

Planting and nurturing plants is a wonderful way to feel grounded. Placing your hands in the warm moist soil and watching your flowers blossom is a symbolic way for you to heal.

Drawing

Expressing yourself while taking your mind off your pain is relaxing and creative. Right-brain drawing classes can help you tap into your creative source. Everyone has this source within. At first you may find class exercises awkward, but you will soon see improvement in your drawings.

Playing an Instrument

Focusing on playing an instrument releases energy and engages your mind. Albert Einstein played his violin for relaxation. Thomas Jefferson was another who found solace through his music. If you have never taken up a musical instrument, you may wish to begin now.

Cooking

A friend of mine who is an adult survivor of incest is a wonderful baker. She gives away most of what she bakes, but she derives great pleasure from her skills. Another survivor creates delicious soups. She stocks her freezer with chicken soup for friends who are feeling sad or ill.

Massage

A full body massage is a great way to relax and loosen tight muscles. There are specialists in the body-work field who focus on particular techniques to enhance the flow of energy throughout your body.

~

You can draw on a number of helping resources as you face your childhood fears. When you practice them, you may discover that your anchors also assist you in developing healthy coping styles. They can be accessed during periods of panic or pockets of craziness moments.

Healing:

The Promise at the End of the Puzzle

Adult survivors of incest can and do heal from their early experience. It is one of the wonderful comments on the human being's power of spirit and resiliency.

When incest survivors begin their recovery work, one of the questions they ask most frequently is "How long will this take?" Another is "How will I know when I've finished with the work?" You may find comfort in knowing that you share many of your concerns with others.

How long will the healing process take, and how will I know when I've finished?

Healing takes a lifetime, but the joy is in the journey, and each stage along the way has its rewards. But to be more specific, you will know when your difficult work is finished because you will have integrated within yourself the following changes in your feelings or behavior.

The Promise of Recovery

Your times of extreme anxiety or those pockets of craziness have subsided to the extent that you are no longer driven by them. They come less frequently and are further apart. You have examined your gatekeepers and let go of most of those that have kept you from living a self-affirming life. You notice a change in your reaction to stress, and when you do begin to feel the panic moments you are able to redirect your energies into productive self-nurturing behavior.

You can ask for help from others and know when you are capable of taking care of your pain by yourself. In other words, you know your needs. And you are comfortable with your support team, a new community of love and nurturing.

You have let go of trying to control people and events. You have learned that no one can be controlled, which also causes you to lighten up on yourself. You shrug off disappointments without running yourself "over the coals."

You set boundaries for yourself. You can say no when you believe that something is not good for you. You can pace yourself, meaning that you do not feel as though your life is out of control. You have self-discipline.

You invite people into your life, rather than being led by them. The nature of your friendships is healthy. You are able to distinguish those who are caring and supportive from those who wish to revictimize you.

You can sustain healthy love relationships, understanding that mutual respect requires setting boundaries and a willingness to trust.

You can talk about your incest experience without feeling dizzy or otherwise ill. You can discuss it from an adult point of view without emotion. However, you must experience the emotion before you can discuss the abuse without becoming upset. Don't confuse your initial denial with your recovery.

You are able to enjoy the moment. And you find pleasure in a variety of ways. You can work through a problem without necessarily obsessing about it. You give yourself permission to watch a sunset and enjoy a good book or a nice walk.

Your outlook on life is optimistic. You have begun to think of your cup as being half full rather than half empty. You choose to surround yourself with things you like and face each day knowing that what is best for you will happen for you. Your problems are opportunities to learn rather than obstacles to overcome.

You may forgive the people in your life who hurt you. In order to get to this point in recovery, though, you will have expressed your anger and disappointment. You may have confronted those who were hurtful, but their response was not as significant as your good feeling about dealing directly with your pain.

You can take an objective stance about your problems rather than becoming immersed in them. You have the ability to watch situations unfold rather than become swallowed up by them.

You no longer feel shame or humiliation. You enjoy and appreciate your body and are becoming comfortable with your sexuality as you express it positively.

You have become reacquainted with your inner child. You have learned that she was very strong and in no way responsible for her abuse. She has taught you much about play and self-acceptance. You have, however, become the adult your inner child has sorely needed to be in charge. You feel now that you are one and the same.

As you work through your healing, you will come to understand yourself very well. You are a wealth of information and resources. You are your own strength. You have the ability to change your beliefs and behavior.

You sometimes feel frustration when you experience another, and yet another, panic attack. And you feel discouraged when you hit a new low after remembering another early abuse. But it is also important to know that *your recovery work does take time*. In an era of fast transportation, instant mashed potatoes, and credit cards, it can be difficult to learn patience. But the incest recovery process will assuredly teach you this very necessary trait.

You will learn that good therapy is not painless therapy. And you will come to accept that you may not heal to the extent that you never have to think of your incest again. You will recognize that your incest is very much a part of the person you are.

At times you will be challenged to face your fears once more, as life's problems bring you new opportunities to learn about your abandonment and death issues. Healing can be accomplished in a few years, but growing, a lifetime occupation, is never completed.

Vision for the Future

By reading through the information in this book, you have taken a necessary step in putting together your incest puzzle. You are fortunate that help is available to those who were sexually abused as children.

Take advantage of this opportunity to learn about yourself, and do not be afraid of the unknown. What has been frightening you may be the key you have needed to unlock your higher potential.

Use your incest recovery to become more forgiving of yourself, more sensitive to the trials of humankind, and more earnest in your pursuit of a healthier world. As a popular bumper sticker states, "In the becoming is everything." The result of your labor is not bad, either.

I wish you luck on your journey.

Appendix: Investigation and Recovery Process Exercises

Here are some exercises designed to help you along the path to recovery. Remember that this journey should be gentle and nurturing, so approach this work with compassion for yourself. Proceed at a pace that feels right for you, and remember that recovery is a process.

Exercise 1: Triggers, Panic Attacks (Fears), and Gatekeepers (Defenses)

Take a piece of paper and make three columns listing your triggers, the fears they cause to surface, and how you defend yourself against them. Use the following as examples:

Trigger	Fear	Defense
Sleep	Nightmares	Sleeping pills
Lovemaking	Violation	Withdrawal
"I love you"	Abandonment	Anger

Exercise 2: Piecing Together the Puzzle

This is an opportunity to list your personal puzzle pieces. Remember that you may need to add to this list as time goes by and you remember more of your past.

Adult Behaviors

sample: mood swings

1.

2.

3.

4.

5.

Family of Origin

sample: assumed caretaker role

1.

2.

3.

4.

5.

Childhood Memories of Your Behaviors and Physical Ailments

sample: compulsively pulled out hair

1.

2.

3.

4.

5.

Intuitions, Flashbacks, or Vague Recollections

sample: hazy memory of being held down and fondled

1.

2.

3.

4.

5.

Exercise 3: Finding Harmony or Balance

Each of us is in search of a balanced life, but many of us focus on one aspect of our lives to the detriment of others. Thus some people become super athletic but forget the need for intellectual development, while others focus on emotional development while forgetting the importance of spiritual practice. Many of us focus on our careers and fail to develop our capacity for intimacy in relationships.

Try this helpful exercise to assess your current state of well-being. Draw a large circle, making a pie graph with six sections. In each section, list how you are balancing your life in the following areas: physical health, spirituality, relaxation, work, emotions, and relationships. Now examine your completed circle. It is balanced in all these areas?

You may find that you are not in harmony with all areas of your life. Make a plan for developing those neglected areas. The plan might include practicing meditation if you feel the lack of spiritual growth, exercise if you are lacking in the physical aspect, or therapy if you are lacking intimacy in relationships.

Exercise 4: Personal Recovery Contract

Commitment is the key to recovery. Many of us have spent our energy helping others to the exclusion of our own needs. We often put ourselves at the bottom of our list of priorities. Writing and signing a personal recovery contract is an important statement of self-worth. To assist you in making a commitment to your recovery work, you may wish to sign the personal contract provided below or make up another of your own. In either case, making a personal recovery contract is a positive step toward wellness.

I, _____, am an adult survivor of incest. I acknowledge that as a child I was hurt through no fault of my own. I now wish to make a commitment to recovery from my childhood trauma. In doing so, I am reclaiming my self and embracing my inner child.

Signature _____ Date _____

Exercise 5: Exorcising Your Anger

Facing your anger is an important part of taking back your personal power. Conquering your anger can be very powerful and needs to be carried out with care and respect. Always make sure you are in a safe environment while doing this work and that trusted members of your support team are present. Remember that while the feelings are strong, they will not overcome you. You will be able to express your rage without hurting yourself or others.

1. With a friend present, sit in a chair in a quiet place and imagine your childhood molester is sitting opposite you. Begin to speak aloud to the imagined person, letting him/her know your pain and anger. Tell this person that you have suffered because of what he/she did. Be sure to let this imagined someone know that you are not emotionally dead from the abuse. Let this person know that your spirit will never be broken. Let him/her also know that you have survived beyond your suffering.

2. Create a native American warrior dance while chanting a song of anger and defiance. Stamp your feet and imagine your-

self in battle with your molester. As your chanting rises envision yourself overpowering your aggressor and driving him/her away.

3. Gather together specific objects that remind you of your pain and suffering. Tie them together in cloth and burn them in a safe manner. As you watch the fire, allow your determination and drive to build as you imagine a white fire within your heart consuming all your sorrow. End this ceremony by singing your own song of victory.

Exercise 6: Exorcising Your Shame

Shame is another strong feeling in adult survivors of incest. It serves to prevent the survivor from facing the reality that some-one she trusted chose to betray her. It is important to realize your shame for how it has affected your sense of well-being and self-esteem. To feel ashamed is to feel disgraced. Remember that nothing you did provoked your childhood molestation. The fol-lowing exercises were created to help you exercise this negative feeling.

Record the following story in your own voice and play it back while you are resting in a comfortable position where you feel completely safe.

~

Once upon a time, there was a beautiful little baby deer. She lived in the woods with her mother and loved to play all day with the other baby animals. One day while the baby deer was playing, she wandered farther away than usual from her play area. Quite by accident she found herself in a very dark and scary part of the woods. She looked up from her play and discovered she did not know how to find her way home. She became frightened and began to cry.

Quite suddenly, a black wolf appeared and said to the little deer, "Little deer, how did you get so lost? Are you not fright-ened to be here in these woods all by yourself? You must be a very foolish animal, indeed. You are fortunate that today I have eaten my fill, or you would be my next meal." With that, the wolf crept away. Shaking with fear, the little deer wished that she had not wandered so far away from home.

A short time later, a snake crawled out from under a bush and said, "Little deer, why are you here in this dark wood without your mother? You must be a foolish child, indeed. You are very lucky, because today I have had my fill and so I will not swallow you whole." The snake slithered away. The little deer began to cry again, because she thought she must be a foolish child to have gotten herself into such a dangerous situation. She felt ashamed.

Just then, an owl appeared. He flew down to where the baby deer lay crying and said, "Little deer, why are you crying? You did nothing wrong. You were behaving just as children often do and you forgot yourself in play. There is nothing wrong with behaving as a child, because you still are little. Come, I will lead you out of the wood to your mother." With that, the owl flew into the air and guided the little deer back home.

The baby deer's mother was very happy to see her child. She thanked the owl and kissed her little one. From then on, the baby deer's mother kept a more watchful eye on her child, and the baby felt safe once more.

Take time to view and appreciate your body. Do this gradually, first reviewing your reflection in the mirror while you are dressed in your favorite clothing. Slowly then, take time to stop and observe your body when you are wearing undergarments. Later, view yourself wrapped in a bath towel. Finally, allow yourself to observe yourself nude. When you are able to view yourself without clothing take some minutes to admire your various body parts without interjecting negative thoughts. Thank yourself for having the courage to begin to love your human form.

Write yourself a story or poem and title it, "I am not ashamed." Here is one survivor's poem:

I am not ashamed to see
    what I have been rejecting all these years.

I will not yield again my power to anyone
    because of the shame.

Am I not a person entitled to love, acceptance
    and joy?

Shame is simply a feeling
    One which is fading away.

Notes

Chapter 1. Working the Puzzle

1. Louise De Salvo, *Virginia Woolf: The Impact of Childhood Sexual Abuse on Her Life and Work* (Boston: Beacon Press, 1989).

Chapter 2. Recalling Earlier Times

1. Nancy Davis, Ph.D., *Once Upon a Time . . . Therapeutic Stories to Heal Abused Children* (Oxon Hill, Md.: Nancy Davis, 1988), 14.

Chapter 4. Adult Survivors of Incest

1. Richard D. Krugman, "Recognition of Sexual Abuse in Children," *Pediatrics in Review*, 8, no. 1 (July 1986).

Chapter 5. Pockets of Craziness and Gatekeepers

1. Daniel Goleman, "Key to Post-Traumatic Stress Lies in Brain Chemistry," *New York Times*, June 12, 1990.
2. Ibid.

Chapter 6. Examining Your Puzzle

1. Ellen Bass and Laura Davis, *The Courage to Heal* (New York: Harper & Row, 1988).

Chapter 12. Other Recovery Tools

1. Ellen Bass and Laura Davis, *The Courage to Heal* (New York: Harper & Row, 1988).
2. Brian Weiss, *Many Lives, Many Masters* (New York: Simon & Schuster, 1988).

3. Ellen Ratner, *The Other Side of the Family* (Deerfield Beach, Fla.: Health Communications, Inc., 1990); Marsha Oliver Utain, *Scream Louder* (Health Communications, Inc., 1989); Patricia O'Gorman and Oliver-Diaz, *Twelve Steps to Self-Parenting* (Health Communications, Inc., 1988).

Bibliography

Bass, Ellen, and Laura Davis. *The Courage to Heal: A Guide for Women Survivors of Child Sexual Abuse.* New York: Harper & Row, 1988.

Black, Claudia. *It Will Never Happen to Me.* Denver: M.A.C., 1982.

Bradshaw, John. "Bradshaw On Healing the Shame that Binds You." Deerfield Beach, Fla.: Health Care Communications, Inc., 1988.

Courtois, Christine A. *Healing The Incest Wound: Adult Survivors in Therapy.* New York: W.W. Norton, 1988.

Daugherty, Lynn. *Why Me?* Racine, Wis.: Mother Courage Press, 1984.

Davis, Nancy. *Once Upon a Time: Therapeutic Stories to Heal Abused Children.* Oxon Hill, Md.: Published by the author, 1988.

De Salvo, Louise. *Virginia Woolf: The Impact of Childhood Sexual Abuse on Her Life and Work.* Boston: Beacon Press, 1989.

Ellenson, Gerald S. "Detecting a History of Incest: A Predictive Syndrome." *The Journal of Contemporary Social Work* (November 1985).

Erikson, Erik H. *Childhood and Society.* New York: W.W. Norton, 1963.

Finklehor, D. *Sexually Victimized Children.* New York: Free Press, 1979.

Forward, Riane, and Craig Buck. *Betrayal of Innocence: Incest and Its Devastation.* New York: Penguin Books, 1979.

Freud, S. *Complete Psychological Works.* London: Hogarth Press, 1959.

Gil, Eliana. *Treatment of Adult Survivors of Childhood Abuse.* Walnut Creek, Calif.: Launch Press, 1988.

Goleman, Daniel. "Key to Post-Traumatic Stress Lies in Brain Chemistry." *New York Times* (12 June 1990).

Greist, John H., and James W. Jefferson. *Depression and Its Treatment.* New York: Warner Books, 1984.

Groth, Nicholas. *Men Who Rape: The Psychology of the Offender.* Lexington, Mass.: Lexington Books, 1979.

Hagans, Kathryn B., and Joyce Case. *When Your Child Has Been Molested: A Parents' Guide to Healing and Recovery.* Lexington, Mass.: Lexington Books, 1988.

MacFarlane, Kee, and Jill Waterman. *Sexual Abuse of Young Children.* New York: Guilford Press, 1986.

O'Gorman Oliver-Diaz, Patricia. *Twelve Steps to Self-Parenting.* Deerfield Beach, Fla.: Health Communications, Inc., 1988.

Ratner, Ellen. *The Other Side Of the Family.* Deerfield Beach, Fla.: Health Communications, Inc., 1990.

Satir, Virginia. *Conjoint Family Therapy: A Guide To Theory and Technique.* Palo Alto, Calif.: Science and Behavior Books, 1967.

Sgroi, Suzanne. *Handbook of Clinical Intervention in Child Sexual Abuse.* Lexington, Mass.: Lexington Books, 1982.

Utain, Marsha Oliver. *Scream Louder.* Deerfield Beach, Fla.: Health Communications, Inc., 1989.

Vander Kolk, Charles. "The Trauma Spectrum: The Interaction of Biological and Social Events in the Genesis of the Trauma Response." *Journal of Traumatic Stress* 1, no. 3 (1988).

Whitfield, Charles L. *Healing the Child Within.* Deerfield Beach, Fla.: Health Communications, Inc., 1987.

Woititz, Janet G. *The Struggle For Intimacy.* Deerfield Beach, Fla.: Health Communications, Inc., 1985.

About the
Author

Kathryn Brohl, M.A., is a licensed marriage and family therapist and coauthor of the book, *When Your Child Has Been Molested: A Parents' Guide to Healing and Recovery.* Formerly the director of a comprehensive treatment program for child and adolescent incest survivors, Ms. Brohl maintains a private practice in Miami, Florida. She also presents training seminars for mental health professionals as well as retreats for adult survivors of incest.